An Easy-to-Digest Exploration of Africa's Complex Realities

THE DARK DESTINY OF AFRICA

Navigating Challenges, Forging Hope

OSMAN KARAKAS

2023

About Book

Book Title: **THE DARK DESTINY OF AFRICA**

Navigating Challenges, Forging Hope

Type: Digital E-Book

Format: **PDF**

Size: 6X9 inches - 15.24X22.89 cm

Total Pages: **195**

E-mail: okarakas@hotmail.com

Web: www.osmankarakas.com

CONTENTS

Preface

In the shadows of history, Africa stands as a continent of remarkable diversity, untapped potential, and enduring resilience. The pages that follow offer an unfiltered exploration of the challenges and complexities that have defined Africa's trajectory, casting a light on the often obscured struggles that have shaped its destiny. "The Dark Destiny of Africa: Navigating Challenges, Forging Hope" is not merely a collection of facts and figures; it is a journey into the heart of a continent where history, geopolitics, and aspirations collide.

In these pages, we unveil the intricate web of influences that have perpetuated a reality where Africa's rich natural resources stand in stark contrast to the hardships experienced by its people. We delve into the remnants of colonial legacies, as the echoes of history reverberate through modern dynamics. We uncover the harsh realities of economic struggles, resource mismanagement, and political instability that continue to grip the continent.

Throughout this exploration, the reader will encounter narratives of displacement, migration, and the indomitable spirit of African communities seeking better lives amidst adversity. We peel back the layers to reveal the puppeteers of power, the corruption that corrodes progress, and the challenges of unity across diverse ethnicities and regions.

But woven into these tales of darkness is a thread of hope that remains unbroken. We shine a light on the grassroots movements, the visionaries, and the individuals who are tirelessly working to reshape Africa's narrative. Amidst the shadows, we uncover stories of resilience, progress, and the unwavering determination to forge a brighter path.

As you embark on this journey, let the stories, insights, and realities shared within these pages serve as an invitation to understand, reflect, and engage with the multifaceted layers of Africa's destiny. It is a journey that invites us to acknowledge the complexities of the past, confront the challenges of the present, and envision a future that breaks free from the shadows.

May this book inspire you to see beyond the surface, to challenge assumptions, and to join hands in crafting a narrative that transcends the darkness, illuminating the path toward a more hopeful destiny for Africa and its people.

Osman Karakas

Introduction: Unveiling Africa's Dark Destiny

In the annals of history, Africa has been a continent of complexity, contradiction, and untold stories. It is a land where ancient traditions interweave with modern aspirations, where natural abundance coexists with overwhelming challenges, and where the echoes of past struggles still reverberate in the present. As we embark on a journey through the pages of "The Dark Destiny of Africa: Navigating Challenges, Forging Hope," we are invited to peer beyond the veneer and into the intricate tapestry that has shaped the fate of a continent.

Africa, with its diverse nations, cultures, and landscapes, has long captured the imagination of the world. Yet, beneath the surface lies a reality that is often overshadowed by the narratives of discovery, adventure, and triumph. In these pages, we confront the difficult truths and grapple with the profound complexities that have marked Africa's post-colonial journey.

This book is a testament to the resilience of African nations and their people, who continue to strive for progress despite the weight of historical burdens and ongoing challenges. It is a tribute to the visionaries, activists, and individuals who work tirelessly to redefine Africa's destiny, pushing against the currents of adversity to pave a path toward a more equitable and prosperous future.

In the chapters that follow, we traverse a landscape where neo-colonial dynamics persist, economic struggles intersect with abundant resources, and governance is often marked by autocracy and corruption. We delve into the refugee crisis and the displacement of communities seeking refuge from hardship, and we examine the fractures within nations caused by ethnic conflicts and regional tensions.

Yet, within the darkness, there are sparks of hope that illuminate the way forward. Grassroots movements, civil society initiatives, and the enduring spirit of African communities offer glimpses of what is possible when determination meets opportunity. These stories remind us that Africa's journey is not defined solely by challenges, but also by the collective will to shape a destiny that reflects the aspirations of its people.

As we navigate the pages ahead, we invite you to engage with the stories, insights, and reflections that encapsulate Africa's complex reality. We encourage you to question preconceptions, to seek understanding, and to join in the ongoing discourse about Africa's path. Through exploration and understanding, we hope to unearth a narrative that transcends the shadows, forging a future of shared progress, unity, and hope.

Author

THE DARK DESTINY OF AFRICA

forging a future of shared progress, unity, and hope.

Author

Chapter 1: Echoes of the Past - Tracing the Legacy of Slavery

Introduction:

Understanding the historical context of Africa's struggles

Africa's struggles are deeply rooted in its history, a history shaped by both its triumphs and its profound traumas. To comprehend the challenges that persist on the continent today, one must venture back through time, traversing the corridors of an era marked by darkness and exploitation: the transatlantic slave trade.

The introduction of this chapter sets the stage for our journey, offering a glimpse into the forces that have cast a shadow over Africa's destiny. As we delve into the echoes of the past, we illuminate how the legacy of slavery continues to reverberate through the social, economic, and cultural fabric of African societies.

The transatlantic slave trade, an institution that spanned centuries, is not merely a historical footnote; it is a foundational chapter in Africa's narrative, leaving indelible marks on the continent's present-day realities. By understanding the historical context of this painful era, we can fathom the complexities that have played a pivotal role in shaping Africa's struggles for autonomy, dignity, and prosperity.

Through historical records, narratives of survivors, and scholarly analysis, we aim to paint a comprehensive picture of the impact of slavery on African societies and their descendants. We invite you to journey with us into the heart of history, where the echoes of the past provide essential context for unraveling the challenges and triumphs that lie ahead in our exploration of "The Dark Destiny of Africa."

In this chapter, we lay the groundwork for a deeper understanding of the complexities that have influenced Africa's trajectory, offering a lens through which we can begin to untangle the threads of a legacy that persists to this day.

A brief overview of the transatlantic slave trade and its lasting impact:

The transatlantic slave trade, an infamous chapter in human history, left an indelible mark on Africa, the Americas, and Europe. This chapter provides a succinct overview of this tragic and harrowing trade, tracing its origins, mechanics, and the profound consequences that continue to reverberate through the fabric of societies to this day.

Emerging in the 15th century, the transatlantic slave trade represented a brutal intersection of economic ambitions, colonial expansion, and the dehumanization of millions. African men, women, and children were captured, often forcibly, and subjected to unimaginable hardships as they were transported across the Atlantic Ocean to the Americas. The cruelty and inhumanity that characterized this trade cannot be overstated, as lives were uprooted, families were torn apart, and entire communities were devastated.

The impact of the transatlantic slave trade was felt across continents. In Africa, communities were destabilized, cultures were disrupted, and economies were distorted. The loss of able-bodied individuals had far-reaching consequences, affecting labor forces and impeding development. In the Americas, the legacy of slavery is woven into the social, economic, and cultural fabric, shaping the foundations of nations and influencing power dynamics.

Beyond its direct effects, the transatlantic slave trade contributed to the entrenchment of racial hierarchies, fueling prejudice and systemic inequalities that persist to this day. The dehumanization of enslaved Africans and the brutal treatment they endured laid the groundwork for deeply rooted prejudices that challenge societies in various ways.

Understanding the transatlantic slave trade requires confronting uncomfortable truths about humanity's capacity for cruelty, greed, and the subjugation of others. Acknowledging this history is essential for comprehending the complexities of Africa's present-day struggles, as the echoes of this trade continue to impact economic, social, and political landscapes.

As we delve into "The Dark Destiny of Africa," the legacy of the transatlantic slave trade serves as a foundational lens through which we interpret the interwoven challenges faced by African nations. It underscores the importance of examining history to comprehend the ongoing narratives that shape the continent's path.

In the following chapters, we will explore how the legacy of the transatlantic slave trade intersects with modern dynamics, illustrating the complexity of Africa's trajectory in a world still grappling with the aftermath of historical atrocities.

The scars of slavery on African societies

Social, economic, and cultural consequences

The transatlantic slave trade cast a long shadow over African societies, leaving behind enduring scars that cut across the realms of social, economic, and cultural life. This chapter delves into the multifaceted consequences of slavery, examining how its brutal legacy has shaped the very fabric of African nations.

Social Consequences: Shattered Communities and Fragmented Identities

The social consequences of slavery are profound and far-reaching. Families were torn apart as loved ones were forcibly separated, leading to the disintegration of close-knit communities. The psychological trauma inflicted upon generations of Africans resonates in the present day, influencing interpersonal relationships, notions of self-worth, and collective memory.

Economic Disruptions: Labor Exploitation and Development Setbacks

The economic fabric of African societies underwent a seismic shift due to the transatlantic slave trade. Enslaved individuals were subjected to brutal labor exploitation, driving wealth accumulation in distant lands at the expense of African prosperity. The loss of a significant portion of the labor force hindered economic development and hindered the growth of industries and infrastructure.

Cultural Transformations: Erosion and Resilience

Cultural heritage is a cornerstone of any society, and the scars of slavery run deep in this realm. Many aspects of African cultures were suppressed or distorted during the era of slavery. However, despite the attempts to erase identities, cultural resilience emerged as a powerful force. African traditions, languages, and artistic expressions persist, serving as a testament to the enduring spirit of the continent.

The echoes of slavery are not isolated events consigned to history; they have become a part of Africa's ongoing narrative. Understanding the social, economic, and cultural consequences of slavery is crucial for comprehending the complex tapestry of challenges that African nations confront today. As we navigate through the chapters of "The Dark Destiny of Africa," these consequences will serve as a touchstone, illuminating the broader context in which Africa's struggles for autonomy, justice, and progress unfold.

Chapter 2: The Persistent Colonial Shadow - Neo-Colonial Dynamics

The lingering influence of former colonial powers on independent African nations

The departure of colonial powers from African shores marked a significant turning point in the continent's history, heralding the era of independence. However, as African nations reclaimed their sovereignty, they found themselves ensnared in a web of neo-colonial dynamics that perpetuated the grip of external influences.

Unraveling the intricate tapestry of neo-colonialism, we examine how former colonial powers and international actors have maintained their hold over the destinies of African nations. From economic dependencies to political maneuvering, the echoes of historical subjugation continue to reverberate through contemporary power dynamics.

Economic Dependencies: The Chains of Resource Exploitation

Neo-colonialism often manifests through economic channels, as African nations grapple with a legacy of resource exploitation. The rich natural resources that have long been coveted by external powers have paradoxically become both a blessing and a curse. Despite newfound independence, African economies remain tightly bound to the demands of global markets, perpetuating a cycle of economic subjugation.

Political Machinations: Puppeteers of Sovereignty

The struggle for true political autonomy is further complicated by the insidious manipulation of governance structures. Former colonial powers and international organizations often exert influence over political leaders, shaping policies and decisions that serve their interests. The sovereignty that was fought for and won can be compromised by the subtle maneuvers of external actors.

Cultural Colonization: The Battle for Identity

Neo-colonialism is not limited to the economic and political spheres; it also extends to the realm of culture. The cultural imperialism that accompanied the colonial era still casts its shadow over African societies. The influx of foreign media, consumerism, and ideologies often dilutes and distorts local cultures, further eroding the agency of nations striving to define their own paths.

The legacy of colonialism, once embodied by physical borders and occupation, now presents itself as a complex network of economic, political, and cultural ties that bind African nations to external powers. Understanding the nuances of neo-colonial dynamics is essential for comprehending the challenges faced by African nations in their pursuit of true sovereignty and self-determination.

Economic dependencies and resource exploitation by foreign countries

The intricate web of economic relationships between African nations and foreign powers has had far-reaching consequences on the continent's development and autonomy. This section delves into the mechanisms of economic dependencies and the exploitation of Africa's valuable resources by external countries.

A Complex Nexus of Interdependence

Economic dependencies emerge as a result of historical ties, trade agreements, and investment relationships. While foreign countries often present themselves as partners for development, the reality is often more complex. African nations, despite their sovereign status, find themselves reliant on external actors for crucial resources, technology, and investments, which can perpetuate an unequal balance of power.

Resource Exploitation: A Blessing or a Curse?

Africa's rich natural resources have attracted the attention of foreign countries for centuries. However, the exploitation of these resources has not always translated into equitable economic growth for African nations. Foreign corporations and countries have historically benefited from resource extraction, often leaving local economies vulnerable to price fluctuations and environmental degradation.

This section peels back the layers of economic interdependence, revealing the challenges and imbalances that result from these relationships. By shedding light on the mechanisms of economic dependencies and resource exploitation, we aim to provide a deeper understanding of the complexities that shape Africa's economic landscape and its quest for sustainable development and self-sufficiency.

Unraveling the complexities of post-colonial relationships and their consequences

The aftermath of colonial rule saw the emergence of a new chapter in Africa's history, marked by the struggle for independence and the aspiration to forge sovereign paths. However, the vestiges of colonialism persisted in the form of intricate post-colonial relationships, often yielding unintended consequences. This section delves into the multifaceted nature of these relationships and their far-reaching impact.

Navigating Diplomacy and Dependency

Post-colonial relationships between African nations and their former colonizers or international partners are marked by a delicate dance of diplomacy and dependency. On one hand, African countries sought to assert their autonomy and establish mutual relationships with the global community. On the other hand, historical ties and economic dependencies often influenced the dynamics of these relationships.

Struggles for Political Self-Determination

The quest for political self-determination was a central tenet of post-colonial Africa. Yet, navigating the complexities of international politics while safeguarding national interests proved to be a formidable challenge. The consequences of aligning with particular global powers or international organizations shaped not only foreign policy but also internal dynamics, sometimes exacerbating divisions and conflicts within nations.

Economic and Development Paradigms

Post-colonial relationships also impacted economic and development paradigms in African countries. The lure of foreign investments and aid often came with conditionalities that shaped policy decisions and economic trajectories. These conditionalities, while intended to promote development, at times led to imbalances, debt burdens, and challenges in achieving sustainable growth.

As we unravel the intricacies of post-colonial relationships, we aim to shed light on the nuances that underlie the global interactions that have shaped Africa's destiny. By understanding the consequences of these relationships, we gain insight into the challenges African nations face as they navigate a complex landscape of diplomacy, economic considerations, and the pursuit of self-determination.

Chapter 3: Thirst for Resources - Battling Economic Hardships

The paradox of resource-rich Africa and its economic challenges

In the heart of Africa lies a paradox that has confounded economists, policymakers, and observers alike. It is a continent blessed with an abundance of natural resources, yet plagued by persistent economic hardships. This chapter delves into the enigmatic conundrum of Africa's resource wealth and the economic challenges that continue to haunt its nations.

Abundance in Natural Resources

Africa boasts an unparalleled wealth of natural resources, from minerals and oil to arable land and freshwater reserves. These resources are coveted by the global community and have the potential to fuel economic growth, eradicate poverty, and improve the quality of life for millions of Africans.

The Resource Curse: A Complex Dilemma

Despite this wealth, many African nations grapple with a phenomenon known as the "resource curse." The resource curse is characterized by economic instability, corruption, and inequality, often exacerbated by the mismanagement of resource revenues. Paradoxically, the very resources that should bring prosperity too often lead to conflict and underdevelopment.

Structural Challenges and Global Dynamics

Africa's economic challenges are not solely the result of resource mismanagement. Structural issues, such as weak infrastructure, inadequate education systems, and limited access to healthcare, also play a significant role. Furthermore, the continent's economic fate is intertwined with global dynamics, including fluctuating commodity prices and international trade policies.

As we navigate the complexities of Africa's economic hardships, this chapter aims to illuminate the multifaceted nature of the resource paradox. Understanding the challenges that arise from the continent's wealth in natural resources is essential for charting a path toward economic stability, inclusive growth, and a brighter future for all Africans.

Exploring factors contributing to the continent's economic struggles

The economic challenges faced by African nations are the result of a complex interplay of factors that encompass historical legacies, structural issues, and global dynamics. In this section, we embark on an exploration of these contributing factors, seeking to unravel the intricate web that has shaped Africa's economic landscape.

Historical Legacies: Colonialism and Its Echoes

The echoes of colonialism still resound in Africa's economic struggles. The exploitation of resources, the imposition of artificial borders, and the disruption of traditional economic systems have left indelible marks. Understanding the historical context is crucial for comprehending the enduring challenges African nations face in their quest for economic stability.

Structural Challenges: Weak Infrastructure and Education

Structural challenges within African nations pose significant obstacles to economic growth. Weak infrastructure, inadequate education systems, and limited access to healthcare hinder development efforts. Addressing these issues is essential for building a foundation of human capital and physical infrastructure necessary for sustainable growth.

Global Dynamics: Commodity Prices and Trade Policies

Africa's economic fate is intricately linked to global dynamics. Fluctuating commodity prices, which heavily impact resource-dependent economies, can lead to instability. Trade policies and market access also play a role, shaping the ability of African nations to participate in the global economy on equitable terms.

Governance and Corruption: Impeding Progress

Governance structures and corruption are critical factors in Africa's economic struggles. Weak institutions, lack of transparency, and widespread corruption divert resources away from development and erode public trust. Addressing governance issues is essential for creating an environment conducive to economic progress.

Conflict and Insecurity: Disrupting Stability

Conflict and insecurity, whether driven by ethnic tensions or regional disputes, disrupt economic stability and development efforts. These challenges often lead to displacement, loss of life, and the destruction of critical infrastructure, hindering long-term progress.

Inequality and Access: Bridging the Divide

Economic inequality and limited access to opportunities exacerbate the continent's challenges. Addressing these disparities through inclusive policies and equitable development strategies is essential for ensuring that the benefits of economic growth reach all segments of society.

By exploring these multifaceted factors, we gain insight into the complexities that underlie Africa's economic struggles. It is through a comprehensive understanding of these challenges that African nations, in partnership with the global community, can chart a path toward sustainable economic development and shared prosperity.

Consequences of resource mismanagement on living conditions and prosperity

The mismanagement of Africa's abundant natural resources has had profound repercussions, extending far beyond the economic sphere. In this section, we delve into the tangible consequences that resource mismanagement has on the everyday lives of African citizens and the broader prosperity of the continent.

Economic Instability and Vulnerability

Resource mismanagement often leads to economic instability. Overreliance on resource exports leaves African economies vulnerable to fluctuations in global commodity prices. When prices plummet, governments face revenue shortfalls, which can result in budgetary crises, inflation, and decreased public spending on critical services.

Poverty and Inequality

Resource mismanagement exacerbates poverty and inequality. Despite the potential for resource wealth to alleviate poverty, the benefits are often concentrated in the hands of a few, leaving many marginalized and impoverished. This inequality can fuel social tensions and hinder social cohesion.

Inadequate Social Services

Resource mismanagement can have dire consequences for access to social services. Insufficient investment in education, healthcare, and infrastructure limits opportunities for human development. The lack of quality services further perpetuates the cycle of poverty and hinders individuals from reaching their full potential.

Environmental Degradation

The exploitation of resources without adequate environmental safeguards can lead to severe environmental degradation. Pollution, deforestation, and habitat destruction not only harm ecosystems but also jeopardize the livelihoods of communities that depend on natural resources for their sustenance.

Political Instability and Corruption

Resource mismanagement can contribute to political instability and corruption. The allure of resource revenues often leads to rent-seeking behavior, where political elites and powerful individuals siphon off wealth for personal gain. This undermines democratic institutions and erodes public trust in government.

Social Unrest and Conflict

Resource mismanagement can also fuel social unrest and conflict. Disputes over resource control, unequal distribution of benefits, and grievances related to environmental damage can escalate into violence, destabilizing regions and nations.

Lack of Diversification

Overreliance on a single resource or sector can hinder economic diversification. This lack of diversification leaves economies vulnerable to external shocks and limits opportunities for sustainable growth in other industries.

By examining the consequences of resource mismanagement on living conditions and prosperity, we gain a deeper understanding of the urgent need for responsible and sustainable resource governance in Africa. Addressing these challenges is essential for ensuring that the continent's resource wealth translates into improved living conditions and shared prosperity for all its people.

Chapter 4: Exodus and Displacement - The Refugee Crisis

The push factors driving mass migration and displacement

In this exploration, we delve into one of the most profound humanitarian challenges facing not only Africa but the entire world—the refugee crisis. Millions of individuals and families find themselves uprooted from their homes, compelled to embark on perilous journeys in search of safety, freedom, economic opportunity, or escape from environmental disasters and climate change. This crisis transcends borders and touches the very core of humanity, demanding our collective attention and action.

Conflict and Instability: Fleeing Violence and Insecurity

Conflict and instability are relentless forces that have driven countless Africans from their homes, leaving behind the familiar and the cherished in pursuit of safety and security. Whether ignited by civil wars, regional conflicts, or deep-rooted ethnic tensions, violence forces communities and individuals into the harrowing reality of displacement. Families are torn apart, homes are destroyed, and lives are shattered by the brutality of conflict. The trauma experienced by refugees is immeasurable, and the scars of violence linger long after the initial flight from danger.

Political Oppression and Persecution: Seeking Freedom and Justice

Political oppression and persecution have cast a dark shadow over the lives of many Africans. Dissidents, activists, and marginalized groups face severe repression, often leaving them with no recourse but to embark on treacherous journeys in search of freedom, justice, and a chance to live without fear of persecution. These individuals display remarkable courage in their quest to escape oppression, and their stories underscore the profound importance of safeguarding fundamental human rights.

Economic Hardships and Inequality: Pursuing a Better Life

Economic hardships and stark inequalities drive countless Africans to seek better opportunities beyond their borders. Limited access to jobs, education, and basic services creates an environment where migration becomes not just an option but a lifeline. The allure of a brighter future and the prospect of providing for one's family motivate individuals to undertake arduous journeys, often fraught with danger and uncertainty. The dreams and aspirations of these migrants are powerful reminders of the universal human desire for progress and prosperity.

Environmental Disasters and Climate Change: Escaping Nature's Fury

Africa is increasingly confronting the devastating consequences of environmental disasters and the relentless march of climate change. Droughts, floods, and other ecological challenges render homes uninhabitable, forcing communities to seek refuge in regions where the impact of nature's fury is less severe. This intersection of environmental factors and migration underscores the urgency of addressing climate-related displacement on both regional and global scales. It calls for proactive measures to mitigate the impact of climate change and protect vulnerable populations.

Humanitarian Crises and Resource Scarcity: Navigating Desperation

Humanitarian crises, often exacerbated by resource scarcity, leave populations in desperate need of assistance. Whether due to food shortages, water scarcity, or disease outbreaks, individuals and families are driven to seek refuge in places where the essentials of life—sustenance, clean water, and safety—are more readily available. These crises demand swift and effective humanitarian responses, as they represent a dire manifestation of human suffering and vulnerability.

As we delve into these complex and interconnected push factors, it becomes evident that the refugee crisis is not a single issue but a confluence of many forces, each with its unique challenges and consequences. The lives and experiences of those who have been displaced—often called "forced migrants"—are a testament to the resilience of the human spirit in the face of adversity.

This exploration provides insight into the humanitarian challenges and responses that shape the trajectory of millions of lives. It serves as a call to action, urging the global community to recognize the shared responsibility in addressing the root causes of displacement and in providing refuge and support to those in need. The refugee crisis stands as a profound test of our collective compassion and commitment to the principles of dignity, justice, and human rights. It is a challenge that transcends borders and demands a united and compassionate response from all of humanity.

The plight of African refugees seeking better opportunities abroad

The stories of African refugees are tales of resilience, courage, and hope in the face of adversity. These individuals, often compelled to leave their homes due to conflict, persecution, economic hardships, environmental disasters, or a combination of these factors, embark on arduous journeys in search of better opportunities abroad. Their plight is a stark reminder of the complex challenges that drive mass migration and displacement in Africa and around the world.

Escaping Conflict and Peril

For many African refugees, the journey begins with the desperate need to escape conflict and the imminent dangers it presents. Whether caught in the crossfire of civil wars, facing violence fueled by ethnic tensions, or living under the threat of armed groups, the decision to flee is often a matter of life and death. These individuals leave behind homes and communities shattered by violence, hoping to find safety and security in foreign lands.

Seeking Freedom from Political Oppression

Political oppression and persecution compel many to seek refuge abroad, driven by the desire for freedom and justice. Activists, dissidents, and marginalized groups find themselves at odds with repressive regimes, facing imprisonment, torture, or worse. Their journeys in search of a haven where they can express their beliefs without fear of reprisal reflect the enduring human quest for liberty and the courage to challenge injustice.

Pursuing a Life Free from Economic Hardships

Economic hardships and profound inequalities drive numerous African refugees to pursue opportunities beyond their borders. In regions plagued by limited access to jobs, education, and essential services, migration becomes a lifeline to a better life. Families, often making difficult decisions to leave loved ones behind, embark on journeys filled with hope, determination, and the aspiration for economic prosperity.

Escaping the Fury of Environmental Disasters and Climate Change

As environmental disasters and the impact of climate change become more pronounced in Africa, communities find themselves displaced by nature's fury. Droughts, floods, and other ecological challenges render homes uninhabitable, compelling families to seek refuge in areas less affected by environmental crises. The intersection of environmental factors and migration underscores the urgent need for climate resilience and adaptation strategies.

Navigating Humanitarian Crises and Resource Scarcity

Humanitarian crises, intensified by resource scarcity, leave populations in dire need of assistance. Food shortages, water scarcity, and disease outbreaks drive individuals and families to seek refuge where life's essentials are more accessible. Their journeys reflect the desperation born of circumstances beyond their control, emphasizing the critical importance of humanitarian responses to alleviate suffering and provide hope.

The plight of African refugees represents a human struggle for dignity, security, and a better future. It challenges societies, governments, and the international community to respond with compassion and practical solutions. The resilience and determination of these refugees serve as a powerful testament to the indomitable human spirit, even in the face of immense adversity. Their stories call for solidarity and a commitment to addressing the root causes of displacement while upholding the principles of dignity, justice, and human rights for all.

International responses and the quest for solutions to the refugee crisis

The refugee crisis is a global challenge that transcends borders and demands collective action. As millions of individuals and families are uprooted from their homes due to conflict, persecution, economic hardships, environmental disasters, or a combination of these factors, the international community is called upon to respond with compassion, empathy, and effective solutions. In this exploration, we delve into the multifaceted international responses to the refugee crisis and the ongoing quest for durable solutions.

The Global Context: Understanding the Scale of the Challenge

To comprehend the magnitude of the refugee crisis, it's essential to grasp its global context. Millions of people are forcibly displaced each year, with Africa being one of the continents significantly affected. This crisis calls for a coordinated international effort that goes beyond mere humanitarian assistance to address the root causes and provide pathways to lasting solutions.

Immediate Humanitarian Responses: Providing Lifelines

Humanitarian organizations, both international and local, play a crucial role in providing immediate assistance to refugees. This includes shelter, food, clean water, healthcare, and protection services. Their work is a lifeline for those fleeing conflict and disaster, offering a semblance of security and hope in the midst of chaos.

Resettlement and Asylum: Extending a Helping Hand

Many countries around the world have opened their doors to refugees through resettlement and asylum programs. These initiatives offer a chance for displaced individuals to find safety and rebuild their lives in new communities. However, the global demand for resettlement far exceeds the available places, creating significant challenges for those seeking refuge.

International Organizations: Coordinating Efforts

International organizations such as the United Nations High Commissioner for Refugees (UNHCR) and the International Organization for Migration (IOM) play a central role in coordinating responses to the refugee crisis. They work to ensure the protection of refugees, advocate for their rights, and facilitate partnerships between countries and humanitarian agencies.

Durable Solutions: Beyond Immediate Relief

While immediate humanitarian responses are essential, addressing the refugee crisis requires a long-term perspective. Durable solutions involve efforts to resolve the root causes of displacement and provide pathways for refugees to rebuild their lives with stability and dignity. These solutions include:

1. **Voluntary Repatriation**: When conditions in a refugee's home country improve, they may choose to return voluntarily. Facilitating safe and dignified repatriation is a critical aspect of durable solutions.

2. **Local Integration**: In some cases, refugees may choose to integrate into the host community and build a life in the country where they sought asylum. Local integration involves providing legal status, access to services, and opportunities for self-reliance.

3. **Resettlement**: For those unable to return home or integrate locally, resettlement to a third country becomes an option. This process requires collaboration between host countries, resettlement countries, and international organizations.

4. **Conflict Resolution**: Addressing the root causes of conflicts and working toward peaceful resolutions is fundamental to preventing displacement. Diplomatic efforts, peace negotiations, and international cooperation are essential in this regard.

Challenges and Obstacles: Navigating Complexities

The quest for solutions to the refugee crisis is fraught with challenges and obstacles. These include political tensions, restrictions on access to asylum, resource constraints, and the need for effective coordination among a myriad of stakeholders. Additionally, the protracted nature of many conflicts and crises complicates efforts to find lasting solutions.

The Role of Civil Society: Advocacy and Support

Civil society organizations and advocacy groups are instrumental in raising awareness about the refugee crisis, advocating for policy changes, and providing support to refugees and host communities. Grassroots efforts and the power of collective action contribute to shaping more compassionate and effective responses.

Conclusion: A Global Responsibility

The refugee crisis underscores the collective responsibility of the international community to respond with compassion, solidarity, and effective solutions. While humanitarian assistance remains vital, a more comprehensive approach that addresses root causes and provides durable solutions is imperative. The quest for solutions to the refugee crisis represents a fundamental test of our commitment to upholding the principles of human dignity, justice, and protection for the world's most vulnerable populations.

Chapter 5: Puppeteers of Power - Autocracy and Dictatorship

The rise of autocratic leaders and their impact on governance

In this chapter, we embark on an exploration of a phenomenon that has left an indelible mark on the political landscape of Africa and beyond: the rise of autocratic leaders and their profound impact on governance. From charismatic strongmen to entrenched dictators, these figures have shaped the destiny of nations, leaving a complex legacy of power, authority, and often, controversy.

Understanding Autocracy and Dictatorship: Definitions and Distinctions

Before delving into the narratives of autocratic leaders, it is essential to establish a clear understanding of what constitutes autocracy and dictatorship. Autocracy refers to a system of government where a single leader holds absolute power, making decisions without the consent of the governed. Dictatorship, on the other hand, is characterized by centralized authority, often wielded by a single individual or a small group, typically achieved and maintained through coercion or force.

The Charismatic Strongmen: Populism and Personalization of Power

Many autocratic leaders rise to power through charisma and a populist appeal.

They often position themselves as champions of the people, promising to bring stability, economic growth, and national pride. The charismatic strongman presents a facade of democracy while consolidating power and limiting political competition. Their personalization of power can lead to cults of personality, where the leader's image dominates public life and dissent is stifled.

Entrenched Dictators: The Prolonged Grip on Power

Dictators, in contrast, tend to maintain their rule through authoritarian means, often suppressing political opposition and curtailing civil liberties. Their tenures can span decades, marked by repression, censorship, and the centralization of authority. These entrenched dictators create a climate of fear, where challenging the regime is met with severe consequences.

The Impact on Governance: Erosion of Democratic Institutions

The rise and consolidation of autocratic leaders and dictators have significant implications for governance. Democratic institutions are eroded as checks and balances are weakened or co-opted. The judiciary, media, and civil society often bear the brunt of this assault on democracy. The concentration of power in the hands of a single leader or a small group can undermine the principles of accountability and transparency that are essential for a functioning democracy.

Economic Consequences: The Paradox of Growth and Inequality

Some autocratic leaders boast of economic growth during their tenures, but this growth can be unevenly distributed, leading to stark income inequality. Economic prosperity can mask underlying issues such as corruption, lack of political freedoms, and human rights abuses. Moreover, reliance on a single leader for economic progress can create vulnerabilities, as economic stability is tied to the leader's longevity.

The Role of International Actors: Balancing Interests and Values

The international community often grapples with the challenge of balancing strategic interests with the promotion of democratic values. While some autocratic leaders may be favored by powerful nations for geopolitical reasons, their actions may run counter to the principles of human rights and democracy. This tension highlights the complexities of international diplomacy in the face of autocracy.

The Struggle for Democracy: Opposition Movements and Civil Society

In the face of autocracy and dictatorship, opposition movements and civil society play a critical role in advocating for democratic reforms. These actors, often operating in challenging environments, seek to hold leaders accountable, protect human rights, and promote political pluralism. Their resilience and determination in the face of repression are a testament to the enduring desire for democracy.

Conclusion: Navigating the Path Forward

The rise of autocratic leaders and the endurance of dictators present a complex challenge for governance and democracy. Understanding the dynamics of autocracy and dictatorship is essential for addressing the erosion of democratic values and institutions. The quest for accountable, transparent, and inclusive governance remains a fundamental aspiration, and the struggle for democracy continues in the face of formidable obstacles.

Examining the suppression of democracy, human rights, and freedom of expression

The suppression of democracy, human rights, and freedom of expression is a deeply concerning and pervasive issue that affects societies worldwide. In this comprehensive exploration, we delve into the multifaceted dimensions of this pressing concern, examining the various methods, consequences, and challenges associated with the erosion of democratic values and fundamental freedoms.

Understanding Democracy: Foundations and Principles

Before delving into the suppression of democracy and its related rights and freedoms, it is essential to establish a clear understanding of the foundations and principles of democracy. Democracy is a system of governance characterized by representative institutions, political pluralism, rule of law, and the protection of individual rights and freedoms. Central to democracy are the principles of transparency, accountability, and the participation of citizens in decision-making processes.

Methods of Suppression: Erosion from Within

Suppression of democracy, human rights, and freedom of expression often occurs through a variety of methods, which can be insidious and gradual. These methods include:

1. **Restrictive Legislation**: Governments may enact laws that limit political competition, curtail civil liberties, and restrict the activities of civil society organizations and the media.

2. **Media Control and Censorship**: Suppressing the media's independence and imposing censorship are common tactics employed to control the flow of information and stifle dissent.

3. **Election Manipulation**: Efforts to manipulate elections through gerrymandering, voter suppression, and fraudulent practices undermine the integrity of democratic processes.

4. **Crackdown on Civil Society**: Civil society organizations, which play a vital role in holding governments accountable, are often targeted through legal restrictions, harassment, or even violence.

5. **Restrictions on Freedom of Assembly**: Limiting the right to peaceful assembly hinders citizens' ability to express their grievances and advocate for change.

6. **Judicial Independence**: The erosion of judicial independence can result in politicized courts that fail to uphold the rule of law and protect individual rights.

Consequences of Suppression: The Human Toll

The suppression of democracy and fundamental freedoms has profound consequences for individuals and societies. These consequences include:

1. **Violation of Human Rights**: The erosion of democratic values often leads to widespread human rights abuses, including arbitrary detention, torture, and extrajudicial killings.

2. **Economic Impact**: Lack of transparency and accountability can hinder economic development and discourage investment.

3. **Social and Political Polarization**: Suppression can deepen divisions within society, creating an atmosphere of mistrust and hostility.

4. **Brain Drain**: Talent and expertise may emigrate to countries with greater political freedoms and economic opportunities.

Challenges to International Response: Balancing Interests and Values

The international community often faces challenges in responding to the suppression of democracy and fundamental freedoms. Balancing strategic interests, diplomatic relations, and the promotion of democratic values is a complex and delicate endeavor. However, it is essential to hold governments accountable for their actions and support civil society and activists working to protect democratic principles.

The Role of Civil Society: Defenders of Democracy

Civil society organizations and activists play a crucial role in defending democracy and human rights. Their resilience, advocacy, and commitment to justice often come at great personal risk, yet they remain unwavering in their pursuit of freedom and accountability.

Conclusion: The Imperative of Defending Democracy and Fundamental Freedoms

The suppression of democracy, human rights, and freedom of expression is a grave concern that demands our attention and action. Protecting these fundamental values is not only a moral imperative but also crucial for the well-being and progress of societies. The quest for democracy and the protection of human rights and freedom of expression are ongoing struggles that require collective efforts, both at the national and international levels, to ensure that these principles remain cornerstones of governance and society.

External influences on autocratic regimes and the perpetuation of power

The dynamics of autocratic regimes, characterized by centralized authority, limited political pluralism, and often repressive rule, are complex and multifaceted. One crucial aspect of these regimes that cannot be overlooked is the role of external influences. In this comprehensive exploration, we delve into the intricate web of external factors that shape, sustain, or challenge autocratic regimes around the world, examining the motivations, strategies, and consequences of such influences.

Understanding Autocracy: Characteristics and Variations

Before delving into the external influences on autocratic regimes, it is essential to establish a clear understanding of what constitutes autocracy. Autocratic regimes are characterized by:

1. **Centralized Authority**: Power is concentrated in the hands of a single leader or a small elite group, often with limited checks and balances.

2. **Limited Political Pluralism**: Opposition parties and political competition are often constrained or suppressed.

3. **Restricted Civil Liberties**: Freedom of expression, assembly, and association may be limited or tightly controlled.

4. **Lack of Accountability**: Transparency and accountability mechanisms are often weak or nonexistent.

5. **Authoritarian Rule**: Repression, censorship, and state control over key institutions are common features of autocratic governance.

External Influences: The Motivations and Strategies

External influences on autocratic regimes can take various forms, and their motivations and strategies vary. Some common external influences include:

1. **Economic Interests**: Countries with economic interests in the autocratic regime may seek to maintain stability and favorable economic conditions for their investments and trade relations.

2. **Strategic Alliances**: Autocratic regimes may align themselves strategically with powerful nations for geopolitical reasons, such as access to resources or support in regional conflicts.

3. **Foreign Aid and Assistance**: Autocratic regimes may receive financial and military support from external actors, bolstering their ability to maintain control.

4. **Diplomatic Leverage**: Diplomatic pressure and negotiations may be used by external actors to encourage reforms or human rights improvements within autocratic regimes.

5. **Sanctions and Isolation**: The international community may impose sanctions or isolate autocratic regimes in response to human rights abuses or undemocratic behavior.

Consequences of External Influences: Impact on Governance and Society

The consequences of external influences on autocratic regimes are wide-ranging and complex. These influences can:

1. **Strengthen Autocratic Rule**: Economic and military support from external actors can reinforce the autocratic regime's grip on power.

2. **Foster Dependency**: Extensive external assistance may create dependency, making the regime more resistant to change.

3. **Undermine Legitimacy**: Sanctions and diplomatic pressure can erode the regime's legitimacy, especially if the international community highlights human rights abuses.

4. **Encourage Reform**: Diplomatic negotiations and incentives can encourage autocratic regimes to implement political or economic reforms.

5. **Fuel Repression**: In some cases, external influences may inadvertently empower repressive elements within the regime.

Challenges to External Influence: Balancing Interests and Values

The challenge for external actors is to balance their strategic interests with their commitment to democratic values and human rights. Striking this balance can be complex, especially when geopolitical considerations, economic interests, and national security concerns are at play. International actors often face dilemmas in deciding when and how to engage with autocratic regimes and when to apply diplomatic pressure or sanctions.

The Role of Civil Society: Advocating for Change

Civil society organizations, activists, and grassroots movements play a crucial role in advocating for democratic values and human rights, both domestically and in their engagement with external actors. They often serve as vital bridges between local populations and international organizations or governments, providing insights and perspectives that shape external policies and interventions.

Conclusion: Navigating the Complex Terrain of External Influences

The influence of external actors on autocratic regimes is a complex and multifaceted aspect of international relations. The consequences of these influences can have far-reaching implications for governance, human rights, and the prospects for democratization. Striking the right balance between strategic interests and values is an ongoing challenge for the international community. Ultimately, the pursuit of democratic governance and respect for human rights remains a shared aspiration, requiring careful navigation of the complex terrain of external influences on autocratic regimes.

Chapter 6: Fractured Unity - Ethnic Conflicts and Regional Tensions

The complex interplay of ethnic divisions and regional rivalries

In this chapter, we venture into the intricate and often volatile terrain of ethnic conflicts and regional tensions that have plagued numerous nations. The fractures along ethnic lines and the rivalries between regions are complex phenomena that have profound implications for governance, social cohesion, and the stability of countries. We examine the factors that contribute to these conflicts, their impact on societies, and the potential pathways toward reconciliation and resolution.

Understanding Ethnic Conflicts and Regional Tensions: Definitions and Dynamics

Before delving into the exploration of ethnic conflicts and regional tensions, it is crucial to establish a clear understanding of these terms and their dynamics.

Ethnic Conflicts: These conflicts are rooted in tensions between different ethnic or cultural groups within a nation. They can manifest as violence, discrimination, or political disputes driven by ethnic identity.

Regional Tensions: Regional tensions involve rivalries or disputes between different geographic regions or states within a country. These tensions may revolve around resource allocation, political power, or historical grievances.

Causes of Ethnic Conflicts: Identity, Resources, and Politics

Ethnic conflicts often arise from a complex interplay of factors, including:

1. **Ethnic Identity**: Strong ethnic identities can lead to competition or conflict when groups perceive themselves as distinct and have divergent interests.

2. **Resource Scarcity**: Competition for limited resources, such as land, water, or economic opportunities, can escalate tensions along ethnic lines.

3. **Political Manipulation**: Politicians may exploit ethnic divisions for political gain, exacerbating conflicts for their benefit.

4. **Historical Grievances**: Past injustices, such as colonization or discrimination, can create long-standing grievances that fuel ethnic conflicts.

5. **Nationalism**: Nationalist movements can intensify ethnic conflicts as they seek to assert cultural or ethnic dominance.

The Impact of Ethnic Conflicts: Human Suffering and Instability

Ethnic conflicts have devastating consequences, including:

1. **Loss of Lives**: Violence and conflict-related deaths result in the loss of innocent lives.

2. **Displacement**: Many conflicts force communities to flee their homes, leading to internal displacement or refugee crises.

3. **Economic Disruption**: Conflict disrupts economic activities, causing poverty and instability.

4. **Social Divisions**: Ethnic conflicts deepen social divisions, eroding trust between communities.

5. **Political Instability**: Ethnic conflicts can destabilize governments and hinder the establishment of stable governance structures.

Regional Tensions: Resource Allocation and Political Power

Rivalries between regions within a country often revolve around:

1. **Resource Allocation**: Disputes over access to and control of valuable resources, such as minerals, oil, or agricultural land.

2. **Political Power**: Regional tensions may be exacerbated by competition for political influence or leadership positions within the nation.

3. **Historical Factors**: Historical events or injustices may contribute to regional rivalries.

4. **Cultural Differences**: Cultural distinctions between regions can lead to misunderstandings and tensions.

5. **Economic Disparities**: Economic disparities between regions can fuel resentment and conflict.

Paths Toward Reconciliation and Resolution

Resolving ethnic conflicts and regional tensions is a complex and long-term process that may involve:

1. **Dialogue and Mediation**: Engaging in dialogue between conflicting parties and using mediation to facilitate negotiations.

2. **Conflict Resolution Mechanisms**: Establishing conflict resolution mechanisms and institutions.

3. **Reconciliation Efforts**: Promoting reconciliation and healing through truth and reconciliation commissions, education, and community initiatives.

4. **Political Reforms**: Implementing political reforms that address the root causes of conflicts and ensure equitable representation.

5. **Resource Management**: Developing fair and transparent resource management practices to address resource-related tensions.

Conclusion: Navigating the Complex Terrain of Ethnic Conflicts and Regional Tensions

Ethnic conflicts and regional tensions are complex challenges that require a nuanced understanding and multifaceted solutions. Addressing these issues is essential for fostering social cohesion, political stability, and economic development. Navigating the terrain of ethnic divisions and regional rivalries is a critical endeavor that demands a commitment to dialogue, reconciliation, and equitable governance for the betterment of nations and their diverse populations.

The role of arbitrary borders in perpetuating conflicts and tensions

Introduction: The Significance of Borders

Borders are not mere lines on a map; they are complex socio-political constructs that shape the course of history, define nations, and often influence the dynamics of conflicts and tensions. The purpose of this comprehensive exploration is to delve into the intricate relationship between arbitrary borders and the persistence of conflicts and tensions across the globe. We examine the origins of arbitrary borders, their impact on societies, and the challenges they pose to peaceful coexistence and regional stability.

Defining Arbitrary Borders: Origins and Characteristics

Before we embark on our journey through the role of arbitrary borders, it is essential to establish a clear understanding of what constitutes these borders and their defining characteristics.

Arbitrary Borders: Arbitrary borders refer to political boundaries that are drawn with little regard for the cultural, ethnic, or geographical realities of the affected regions. These borders are often established through colonialism, imperialist ambitions, or geopolitical considerations.

Origins of Arbitrary Borders: Colonialism and Imperialism

Many arbitrary borders find their origins in the colonial and imperialist ambitions of European powers during the 19th and early 20th centuries. The scramble for Africa, the partitioning of the Middle East, and the drawing of borders in Asia often resulted in the creation of nations that did not align with the cultural or ethnic identities of their populations.

Impact on Societies: Fragmentation and Discontent

The impact of arbitrary borders on societies is profound and enduring. Some of the consequences include:

1. **Ethnic and Cultural Fragmentation**: Arbitrary borders can divide ethnic and cultural communities, leading to the creation of nations with diverse populations that may have little in common.

2. **Identity Struggles**: Communities divided by arbitrary borders may experience identity crises, as they grapple with the challenge of belonging to a nation that does not align with their cultural or ethnic identity.

3. **Resource Allocation Disputes**: Borders that cut across valuable resources, such as oil fields or arable land, can lead to disputes and conflicts over resource allocation.

4. **Political Instability**: Nations formed with arbitrary borders may experience political instability as diverse groups vie for power and influence.

Borders as Instruments of Control: Geopolitical Considerations

Arbitrary borders have often served as instruments of control and manipulation by external powers. Geopolitical considerations, such as access to resources, strategic positioning, and regional influence, have driven the drawing of borders that may not align with the interests or desires of the affected populations.

Case Studies: Arbitrary Borders in Action

To gain a deeper understanding of the role of arbitrary borders, we examine several case studies from different regions of the world, including:

1. **The Sykes-Picot Agreement**: The secret agreement between the United Kingdom and France in 1916 that shaped the borders of the modern Middle East.

2. **The Berlin Conference**: The international conference held in 1884-1885 that partitioned Africa among European colonial powers, leading to arbitrary borders.

3. **The Durand Line**: The border between Afghanistan and Pakistan, drawn by British colonial authorities in the 19th century, which continues to be a source of tension.

4. **The Balkans**: The complex web of borders and ethnic divisions in the Balkan region, which contributed to conflicts in the 1990s.

Challenges to Redrawing Borders: The Complex Path to Change

While the consequences of arbitrary borders are evident, the process of redrawing or adjusting borders is fraught with challenges. Some of these challenges include:

1. **Sovereignty Concerns**: Nations are often reluctant to cede territory or redraw borders due to concerns about sovereignty and national identity.

2. **Ethnic and Cultural Complexities**: Determining where new borders should be drawn to align with ethnic and cultural identities can be complex and contentious.

3. **Geopolitical Interests**: Powerful nations may resist changes to existing borders if it goes against their geopolitical interests.

4. **Historical Legacies**: Historical grievances and traumas associated with borders can hinder efforts to redraw them.

Conclusion: The Imperative of Addressing Arbitrary Borders

Arbitrary borders remain a persistent source of conflicts and tensions in the modern world. Understanding their origins, impact, and the challenges of redrawing them is essential for addressing the complexities they pose. While altering borders may be a delicate and contentious process, it is imperative to consider the potential for peaceful resolution and greater alignment with the cultural and ethnic realities of affected populations. Ultimately, the role of arbitrary borders in perpetuating conflicts and tensions calls for a reevaluation of international norms and practices to promote stability, justice, and the peaceful coexistence of nations.

Case studies of conflicts and efforts toward peace and stability

Introduction: The Complex Landscape of Conflicts and Peace

The world has witnessed a multitude of conflicts, large and small, each with its unique dynamics, causes, and consequences. In this extensive exploration, we delve into case studies of conflicts from various regions, examining the underlying factors, the devastating impact on societies, and the relentless efforts toward peace and stability.

Through these in-depth analyses, we aim to gain a deeper understanding of the complexities of conflicts and the resilience of human resolve to seek peaceful resolutions.

Case Study 1: The Rwandan Genocide (1994)

The Rwandan Genocide stands as a stark reminder of humanity's capacity for violence and brutality. In just 100 days, an estimated 800,000 people, primarily of the Tutsi ethnic group, were killed by ethnic Hutu extremists. The conflict had deep-rooted historical and political causes, exacerbated by hate propaganda and international indifference.

Causes:

- **Ethnic Tensions**: Decades of ethnic divisions and tensions between the Hutu and Tutsi communities fueled the conflict.

- **Political Instability**: A history of political instability and power struggles contributed to the crisis.

- **Hate Propaganda**: Radio broadcasts and propaganda campaigns played a significant role in inciting violence.

Efforts Toward Peace:

- **International Intervention**: The international community, criticized for its inaction during the genocide, has since worked to support Rwanda's recovery and reconciliation.

- **Rwandan Reconciliation**: Rwanda has made significant progress in reconciliation efforts, including the use of community courts (Gacaca) to address crimes and promote healing.

Case Study 2: The Israeli-Palestinian Conflict (Ongoing)

The Israeli-Palestinian conflict has spanned decades, with its roots in historical, territorial, and political disputes. It remains one of the most intractable conflicts in the world, marked by violence, tensions, and international mediation efforts.

Causes:

- **Territorial Disputes**: The conflict is centered on competing claims to territory, particularly in the West Bank and Gaza Strip.

- **Historical Tensions**: Decades of historical grievances and conflicts have contributed to deep-seated animosities.

- **Political Complexities**: The involvement of various political actors, including Israel, the Palestinian Authority, and Hamas, adds layers of complexity.

Efforts Toward Peace:

- **Oslo Accords**: The 1993 Oslo Accords marked a significant step toward peace but faced challenges and setbacks.

- **International Mediation**: Numerous international mediation efforts, including the Quartet on the Middle East and the United Nations, have aimed to facilitate peace negotiations.

Case Study 3: The Colombian Civil War (1964-2016)

Colombia's civil war, spanning over five decades, was characterized by violence, insurgent groups, and government forces. The conflict had profound socio-political, economic, and humanitarian consequences.

Causes:

- **Inequality**: Socio-economic disparities and marginalization contributed to the rise of insurgent groups.

- **Drug Trade**: The drug trade, particularly cocaine production, played a significant role in funding armed groups.

- **Political Instability**: Political violence and assassinations were common during the conflict.

Efforts Toward Peace:

- **Peace Negotiations**: The Colombian government engaged in peace negotiations with the Revolutionary Armed Forces of Colombia (FARC) and other armed groups.

- **Demobilization**: Thousands of combatants demobilized, and efforts were made to reintegrate them into society.

Case Study 4: The Troubles in Northern Ireland (1969-1998)

The Troubles in Northern Ireland were marked by sectarian violence, political unrest, and deep-rooted divisions between the Protestant and Catholic communities. The conflict came to an end with the Good Friday Agreement in 1998.

Causes:

- **Religious and Ethnic Divisions**: Sectarian tensions between Protestants and Catholics fueled the conflict.

- **Political Struggles**: Political demands for sovereignty and self-determination contributed to the violence.

- **Economic Disparities**: Economic inequalities exacerbated social tensions.

Efforts Toward Peace:

- **Good Friday Agreement**: The agreement, brokered with international mediation, established a framework for peace and power-sharing.

- **Decommissioning**: Paramilitary groups decommissioned their weapons, contributing to a more stable environment.

Case Study 5: The South Sudan Conflict (2013-ongoing)

The conflict in South Sudan, one of the world's youngest nations, has been characterized by ethnic violence, political disputes, and humanitarian crises. It began shortly after South Sudan gained independence from Sudan in 2011.

Causes:

- **Ethnic Divisions**: Ethnic tensions, particularly between the Dinka and Nuer communities, have played a significant role.

- **Political Struggles**: Political power struggles and disputes between leaders escalated the conflict.

- **Humanitarian Consequences**: The conflict has resulted in widespread displacement and food insecurity.

Efforts Toward Peace:

- **Peace Agreements**: Several peace agreements have been brokered, although they have faced challenges in implementation.

- **International Mediation**: Regional and international actors have been involved in mediation efforts.

Conclusion: Lessons from Conflict and Hope for Peace

These case studies provide a glimpse into the complexities of conflicts and the diverse efforts to achieve peace and stability. While conflicts often arise from deeply ingrained historical, political, and socio-economic factors, the case studies also highlight the resilience of human determination to seek peaceful resolutions. The path to peace is challenging, but these examples remind us that with international cooperation, mediation, and a commitment to addressing root causes, conflicts can be resolved, and societies can heal and rebuild.

Chapter 7: A Fragile Environment - Environmental Degradation and Sustainability

Unveiling environmental challenges facing African countries

Introduction: The Vital Link Between Environment and Development

Africa, with its breathtaking landscapes and diverse ecosystems, is a continent of unparalleled natural beauty and ecological significance. Yet, beneath this striking exterior lies a pressing issue that demands our attention and action - environmental degradation. In this chapter, we embark on a journey to uncover the intricate environmental challenges facing African countries, exploring the complex relationship between the environment, sustainable development, and the well-being of nations.

Defining Environmental Degradation: A Growing Crisis

Before delving into the exploration of environmental challenges, it is essential to establish a clear understanding of what constitutes environmental degradation and its defining characteristics.

Environmental Degradation: Environmental degradation refers to the deterioration of the environment through the depletion of natural resources, pollution, habitat destruction, and other adverse changes that harm ecosystems and disrupt the balance of nature.

Causes of Environmental Degradation: The Human Footprint

Environmental degradation in African countries is driven by a combination of factors, including:

1. **Deforestation**: The clearing of forests for agriculture, logging, and urban development leads to loss of biodiversity, soil erosion, and disrupted water cycles.

2. **Resource Exploitation**: Unsustainable extraction of minerals, oil, and other natural resources can have detrimental effects on local ecosystems and communities.

3. **Pollution**: Pollution from industries, agriculture, and inadequate waste management contaminates air, water, and soil.

4. **Climate Change**: Africa is vulnerable to climate change, with rising temperatures, erratic rainfall, and extreme weather events affecting agriculture and water resources.

5. **Population Growth**: Rapid population growth places increased pressure on land, water, and food resources.

Consequences of Environmental Degradation: Human and Ecological Impacts

The consequences of environmental degradation extend far beyond ecological concerns, encompassing profound human and societal impacts:

1. **Loss of Biodiversity**: Habitat destruction and pollution threaten the rich biodiversity of African ecosystems, leading to the extinction of species.

2. **Food Insecurity**: Environmental degradation disrupts agricultural systems, contributing to food insecurity and malnutrition.

3. **Water Scarcity**: Pollution and mismanagement of water resources lead to water scarcity and inadequate access to clean drinking water.

4. **Health Impacts**: Pollution and environmental degradation contribute to a range of health issues, including respiratory diseases and waterborne illnesses.

5. **Conflict**: Competition for scarce resources, such as water and arable land, can exacerbate conflicts within and between nations.

Sustainable Development: Balancing Growth and Conservation

Sustainable development offers a path forward, seeking to balance economic growth with environmental conservation and social equity. Key principles of sustainable development include:

1. **Environmental Stewardship**: Responsible management of natural resources to ensure their long-term availability.

2. **Economic Prosperity**: Economic development that benefits society while minimizing negative environmental impacts.

3. **Social Equity**: Ensuring that the benefits of development are shared equitably among all segments of society.

4. **Climate Action**: Mitigating and adapting to climate change through sustainable practices and renewable energy sources.

Case Studies: Environmental Challenges Across Africa

To gain deeper insights into the environmental challenges facing African countries, we examine several case studies from different regions:

1. **Deforestation in the Congo Basin**: The impact of deforestation on the world's second-largest rainforest and its role in global climate regulation.

2. **Oil Pollution in the Niger Delta**: The environmental and social consequences of oil extraction in Nigeria's Niger Delta region.

3. **Desertification in the Sahel**: The encroachment of deserts and land degradation in the Sahel region, exacerbated by climate change.

4. **Water Scarcity in the Horn of Africa**: The challenges of water scarcity and resource management in the Horn of Africa, with a focus on Ethiopia and Somalia.

Efforts Toward Sustainability: Conservation and Restoration

Efforts to address environmental degradation and promote sustainability in African countries encompass a range of initiatives:

1. **Conservation**: Protected areas, national parks, and conservation programs are crucial for preserving biodiversity and ecosystems.

2. **Reforestation**: Reforestation and afforestation projects aim to restore degraded lands and combat deforestation.

3. **Renewable Energy**: Investment in renewable energy sources, such as solar and wind power, contributes to sustainable development and mitigates climate change.

4. **Waste Management**: Improved waste management practices reduce pollution and promote cleaner environments.

5. **Community Engagement**: Involving local communities in sustainable practices and resource management is essential for long-term success.

Conclusion: A Call to Action

The environmental challenges facing African countries are complex and multifaceted, but they are not insurmountable. Recognizing the vital link between a healthy environment and sustainable development, there is a collective responsibility to take action. By implementing sustainable practices, conserving natural resources, and addressing the root causes of environmental degradation, African nations can build a brighter, more sustainable future for their people and the planet.

Impact of ecological issues on health, livelihoods, and economic growth

Introduction: The Interconnected Web of Ecology and Human Well-being

The intricate web of ecology, encompassing the natural environment and the delicate balance of ecosystems, is inextricably linked to the well-being of humanity. In this comprehensive exploration, we delve into the profound impact of ecological issues on health, livelihoods, and economic growth, recognizing the intricate relationships that underpin the interconnectedness of our world.

Defining Ecological Issues: A Multifaceted Challenge

Before we embark on our journey to uncover the impact of ecological issues, it is essential to establish a clear understanding of what constitutes these issues and their defining characteristics.

Ecological Issues: Ecological issues encompass a wide range of challenges related to the environment, including biodiversity loss, habitat degradation, pollution, deforestation, climate change, and resource depletion.

The Nexus of Health, Livelihoods, and Economic Growth

Ecological issues are not isolated problems; they ripple through society, affecting health, livelihoods, and economic growth in profound ways.

Impact on Health: The Toll on Human Well-being

Ecological issues have direct and indirect consequences for human health:

1. **Air Pollution**: Poor air quality resulting from industrial emissions and deforestation contributes to respiratory diseases and cardiovascular problems.

2. **Water Contamination**: Polluted water sources lead to waterborne diseases, impacting the health of communities.

3. **Vector-Borne Diseases**: Climate change and habitat disruption can expand the geographic range of disease vectors, such as mosquitoes carrying malaria or dengue fever.

4. **Food Security**: Ecosystem disruptions affect agricultural yields, leading to food insecurity and malnutrition.

5. **Mental Health**: The loss of natural environments can have adverse effects on mental well-being, contributing to stress and anxiety.

Impact on Livelihoods: The Foundation of Communities

Ecological issues profoundly affect the livelihoods of communities:

1. **Agriculture**: Climate change, soil degradation, and water scarcity challenge agricultural productivity, jeopardizing the livelihoods of farmers.

2. **Fisheries**: Overfishing and habitat destruction threaten the livelihoods of coastal communities dependent on fisheries.

3. **Tourism**: Ecosystem degradation diminishes the appeal of natural tourist destinations, impacting the tourism industry and the livelihoods it supports.

4. **Forestry**: Deforestation and habitat loss affect communities reliant on forest resources for their livelihoods.

5. **Urbanization**: Ecological issues, such as inadequate waste management and pollution, can lead to health problems in urban areas, impacting livelihoods and well-being.

Impact on Economic Growth: The Ripple Effect

The consequences of ecological issues reverberate through economies:

1. **Agricultural Productivity**: Declining agricultural yields can lead to reduced food production and increased prices, impacting overall economic stability.

2. **Healthcare Costs**: Increased healthcare expenses due to environmental-related illnesses strain public and private healthcare systems.

3. **Natural Resource Depletion**: Overexploitation of natural resources can undermine long-term economic growth prospects.

4. **Disaster Resilience**: Ecological issues, such as deforestation and climate change, make communities more vulnerable to natural disasters, leading to economic losses.

5. **Investor Confidence**: Ecological risks can erode investor confidence, affecting foreign direct investment and economic development.

Sustainable Solutions: Navigating the Nexus

Navigating the complex nexus of ecological issues, health, livelihoods, and economic growth requires sustainable solutions:

1. **Ecosystem Restoration**: Efforts to restore ecosystems and protect biodiversity are essential for human well-being and sustainable development.

2. **Renewable Energy**: Transitioning to renewable energy sources mitigates climate change and promotes economic growth.

3. **Circular Economy**: Promoting circular economy practices reduces waste and conserves resources, benefiting both the environment and the economy.

4. **Green Infrastructure**: Investing in green infrastructure, such as urban parks and sustainable agriculture, enhances resilience and well-being.

5. **Education and Awareness**: Raising awareness and educating communities about ecological issues and sustainable practices is crucial for fostering positive change.

Case Studies: Unveiling Real-World Impacts

To gain deeper insights into the real-world impacts of ecological issues, we examine case studies from diverse regions:

1. **The Amazon Rainforest**: Deforestation in the Amazon has far-reaching consequences for climate, biodiversity, and indigenous communities.

2. **Air Pollution in Urban Centers**: The health and economic toll of air pollution in rapidly urbanizing areas, such as Delhi, India.

3. **Marine Pollution**: The impact of plastic pollution on marine ecosystems and coastal communities.

4. **Climate Change in Small Island States**: The vulnerability of small island developing states to rising sea levels and extreme weather events.

5. **Agricultural Challenges in Sub-Saharan Africa**: The link between ecological issues, food security, and economic development in the region.

Conclusion: A Holistic Approach to Well-being and Prosperity

The impact of ecological issues on health, livelihoods, and economic growth is a multifaceted challenge that requires holistic solutions. Recognizing the interdependence of ecosystems and human well-being, societies must prioritize sustainability, conservation, and resilience. Only by embracing a comprehensive approach to environmental stewardship can we hope to navigate the nexus of ecology, human health, livelihoods, and economic growth, securing a brighter and more sustainable future for all.

Strategies for sustainable development and environmental conservation

Introduction: The Imperative of Sustainable Development

In an era defined by global challenges, sustainable development and environmental conservation have emerged as not only ethical imperatives but also essential pathways to securing the future of our planet and the well-being of generations to come. In this comprehensive exploration, we delve into the strategies that drive sustainable development and environmental conservation, recognizing their pivotal role in addressing ecological crises and fostering prosperity.

Defining Sustainable Development: A Holistic Vision

Before we embark on our journey to uncover strategies for sustainable development, it is essential to establish a clear understanding of what constitutes sustainable development and its defining characteristics.

Sustainable Development: Sustainable development refers to the pursuit of economic growth, social equity, and environmental protection in a way that meets the needs of the present without compromising the ability of future generations to meet their own needs.

The Pillars of Sustainable Development: A Balanced Approach

Sustainable development rests upon three interconnected pillars:

1. **Economic Prosperity:** Ensuring that economic activities promote growth, job creation, and poverty reduction while maintaining ecological balance.

2. **Social Equity**: Fostering inclusive societies that provide access to education, healthcare, and opportunities for all, addressing disparities in wealth, gender, and social status.

3. **Environmental Conservation**: Preserving and restoring ecosystems, protecting biodiversity, and mitigating the impact of human activities on the environment.

Strategies for Sustainable Development: A Multi-Faceted Approach

Achieving sustainable development requires a multi-faceted approach encompassing various strategies:

1. **Green Growth**: Promoting economic growth through sustainable practices, including renewable energy, eco-friendly technologies, and circular economy principles.

2. **Policy Frameworks**: Implementing policies and regulations that incentivize sustainable practices, such as carbon pricing, renewable energy targets, and emissions reductions.

3. **Education and Awareness**: Raising awareness and educating communities about the importance of sustainability and the consequences of unsustainable practices.

4. **Resource Management**: Ensuring responsible management of natural resources, including

water, forests, minerals, and fisheries, to prevent depletion and degradation.

5. **Community Engagement**: Involving local communities in decision-making processes and sustainable development initiatives to ensure inclusivity and empowerment.

6. **Sustainable Agriculture**: Promoting sustainable farming practices that enhance productivity while conserving soil, water, and biodiversity.

Environmental Conservation Strategies: Safeguarding Ecosystems

Environmental conservation is central to sustainable development, and strategies include:

1. **Protected Areas**: Establishing and maintaining protected areas, national parks, and marine reserves to safeguard biodiversity and ecosystems.

2. **Habitat Restoration**: Restoring degraded habitats through reforestation, afforestation, and wetland restoration projects.

3. **Biodiversity Protection**: Implementing measures to protect endangered species and conserve biodiversity, such as wildlife corridors and conservation easements.

4. **Sustainable Fishing**: Enforcing regulations and practices that promote sustainable fishing and protect marine ecosystems.

5. **Climate Action**: Mitigating climate change through emissions reductions, reforestation, and climate-resilient infrastructure.

Case Studies: Exemplifying Success and Challenges

To gain deeper insights into the real-world application of sustainable development and environmental conservation strategies, we examine case studies from diverse regions:

1. **Costa Rica's Conservation Model**: The success of Costa Rica's protected area system and commitment to biodiversity conservation.

2. **Germany's Renewable Energy Transition**: Germany's "Energiewende" and the transition to renewable energy sources.

3. **The Great Green Wall of Africa**: The ambitious project to combat desertification and land degradation in the Sahel region.

4. **Community-Based Conservation in Namibia**: The communal conservancy program and its positive impact on wildlife and local communities.

5. **The Challenges of the Amazon Rainforest**: The ongoing threats to the Amazon Rainforest and the

need for international cooperation in its preservation.

Challenges and Future Directions: Navigating Obstacles

While sustainable development and environmental conservation hold immense promise, they also face significant challenges:

1. **Short-Term Interests**: The tension between short-term economic interests and long-term environmental sustainability.

2. **Political Will**: The need for strong political will and international cooperation to implement effective policies and regulations.

3. **Resource Scarcity**: The growing challenges of resource scarcity, water scarcity, and food security.

4. **Climate Change**: The urgency of addressing climate change and its far-reaching consequences for the planet.

5. **Inequality**: Addressing disparities in access to resources, education, and opportunities, which are central to sustainable development.

Conclusion: A Shared Responsibility

Strategies for sustainable development and environmental conservation represent a shared responsibility that transcends borders and ideologies. Embracing sustainability as a guiding principle for decision-making, policy formulation, and daily actions is imperative for safeguarding the planet's future. As we navigate the complexities of our interconnected world, the strategies we employ today will shape the legacy we leave for generations to come, emphasizing the critical importance of a sustainable and ecologically conscious future.

Chapter 8: The Corruption Quagmire - Misappropriation and Exploitation

The pervasive issue of corruption in African governments

Introduction: The Shadow of Corruption

Corruption, an insidious force that undermines the trust of citizens, erodes the foundations of governance, and siphons resources away from vital public services, is a pervasive issue that afflicts governments worldwide. In this chapter, we focus on the African context, where corruption has had far-reaching and deeply entrenched consequences, impeding development, fostering inequality, and exacerbating poverty.

Defining Corruption: A Multifaceted Challenge

Before we delve into the exploration of corruption in African governments, it is essential to establish a clear understanding of what constitutes corruption and its defining characteristics.

Corruption: Corruption encompasses a range of dishonest and unethical behaviors, including bribery, embezzlement, nepotism, cronyism, and abuse of power for personal gain. It undermines the integrity of institutions and the public trust.

The Toll of Corruption: An Inescapable Reality

Corruption extracts a heavy toll on societies, economies, and governance systems, resulting in dire consequences that extend far beyond financial losses:

1. **Economic Impacts**: Corruption distorts markets, reduces foreign investment, and stifles economic growth, hindering poverty reduction efforts.

2. **Social Consequences**: It exacerbates inequality, as resources meant for public services are diverted to enrich the corrupt, leaving vulnerable populations without access to education, healthcare, and basic amenities.

3. **Political Instability**: Corruption erodes trust in political institutions and can lead to social unrest and political instability.

4. **Environmental Degradation**: It contributes to environmental destruction through illegal resource exploitation and lax enforcement of environmental regulations.

5. **Loss of Human Capital**: Corruption can drive skilled professionals and entrepreneurs away from countries where opportunities for bribery and embezzlement are prevalent.

Corruption in African Governments: A Complex Landscape

African countries, though diverse in culture, history, and political structures, share common challenges in combating corruption. Several factors contribute to the complex landscape of corruption on the continent:

1. **Historical Legacy**: The legacy of colonialism and authoritarian rule has left a lasting imprint on governance structures, fostering corruption in some cases.

2. **Economic Vulnerability**: Many African nations face economic challenges, making corruption an attractive means of wealth accumulation for individuals in power.

3. **Inadequate Institutions**: Weak and under-resourced institutions are more susceptible to corruption and less able to combat it effectively.

4. **Cultural Factors**: In some cases, cultural norms and practices may inadvertently facilitate corrupt practices.

Case Studies: Corruption Across African Nations

To gain deeper insights into the real-world manifestations of corruption in African governments, we examine case studies from diverse regions:

1. **Nigeria's Battle with Oil Corruption**: The impact of corruption on Nigeria's oil industry and the challenges of combating it.

2. **The Arms Deal Scandal in South Africa**: The controversial arms procurement deal that exposed

high-level corruption and its implications for governance.

3. **The Watergate Scandal in Kenya**: A case study of embezzlement and misappropriation of public funds earmarked for water projects.

4. **Zimbabwe's Decades of Corruption**: The prolonged history of corruption and mismanagement in Zimbabwe and its impact on the economy and political stability.

5. **Botswana's Success in Combating Corruption**: The anti-corruption measures that have contributed to Botswana's relatively low levels of corruption compared to other African nations.

Efforts to Combat Corruption: Challenges and Progress

While corruption remains a deeply entrenched issue, African governments and international organizations have not been passive in their efforts to combat it:

1. **Legislative Reforms**: Many countries have enacted anti-corruption laws and established anti-corruption agencies to investigate and prosecute corrupt individuals.

2. **Civil Society Engagement**: Civil society organizations play a crucial role in raising awareness, advocating for transparency, and holding governments accountable.

3. **International Cooperation**: Initiatives like the United Nations Convention against Corruption (UNCAC) and regional anti-corruption efforts have promoted international cooperation in tackling corruption.

4. **Whistleblower Protection**: Implementing laws and mechanisms to protect whistleblowers who expose corruption.

Challenges and Future Directions: The Long Road Ahead

The fight against corruption in African governments is a long and challenging one, marked by persistent obstacles:

1. **Political Will**: The need for unwavering political will to enforce anti-corruption measures, even when it implicates powerful individuals.

2. **Judicial Independence**: Ensuring that judicial systems are independent and free from political interference is crucial for combating corruption.

3. **Capacity Building**: Strengthening institutions and enhancing their capacity to investigate and prosecute corruption cases.

4. **Public Education**: Raising public awareness about the corrosive effects of corruption and the role citizens can play in demanding accountability.

Conclusion: The Imperative of Transparency and Accountability

The pervasive issue of corruption in African governments is a formidable challenge, but it is not insurmountable. As African nations continue their journey toward development and prosperity, they must prioritize transparency, accountability, and the rule of law. By fostering a culture of integrity, enforcing anti-corruption measures, and engaging civil society, African countries can confront corruption head-on, ensuring that public resources are used for the benefit of all citizens, and that the promise of sustainable development becomes a reality across the continent.

The connection between corrupt leaders, global corporations, and resource sales

Introduction: The Web of Corruption and Exploitation

In the complex landscape of global politics and economics, a troubling connection often emerges - the nexus between corrupt leaders, global corporations, and the sale of a nation's valuable resources. This chapter explores the intricate web of corruption and exploitation that ensnares nations, robbing them of their wealth and leaving their citizens impoverished. It is a story of power, greed, and the betrayal of public trust.

Defining the Nexus: Corruption and Resource Exploitation

Before we unravel the connections between corrupt leaders, global corporations, and resource sales, it is essential to define the key components of this troubling nexus:

Corruption: Corruption encompasses a range of dishonest practices, including bribery, embezzlement, nepotism, and abuse of power, aimed at personal gain or the enrichment of a select few.

Resource Exploitation: The extraction and sale of valuable natural resources, including minerals, oil, gas, and timber, often under the control of governments.

The Mechanisms of Exploitation: How Corruption Takes Root

The connection between corrupt leaders, global corporations, and resource sales often begins with a series of mechanisms that enable exploitation:

1. **Weak Governance**: Fragile institutions and inadequate regulatory frameworks create opportunities for corruption to thrive.

2. **Opaque Contracts**: Secretive contracts between governments and corporations can hide corrupt practices from public scrutiny.

3. **Lack of Accountability**: Insufficient oversight and accountability measures allow those in power to act with impunity.

4. **Resource Dependence**: Nations heavily reliant on resource exports may prioritize short-term gains over long-term sustainable development.

Case Studies: The Global Reach of Corruption

To shed light on the extent and impact of this connection, we examine case studies from various regions:

1. **Nigeria's Oil Curse**: The mismanagement of Nigeria's vast oil wealth and the role of corrupt leaders and international corporations.

2. **Blood Diamonds in Sierra Leone**: The illicit diamond trade in Sierra Leone and its connection to civil conflict and corrupt leaders.

3. **The Timber Mafia in Southeast Asia**: The illegal timber trade in Southeast Asia, driven by corruption and corporate exploitation.

4. **Conflict Minerals in the Democratic Republic of Congo**: The extraction and sale of minerals in a region plagued by conflict and corruption.

5. **Oil and Gas in Venezuela**: The collapse of Venezuela's oil industry and the role of corrupt leadership and global corporations.

Exploitation and Global Corporations: The Pursuit of Profit

Global corporations play a significant role in the nexus between corrupt leaders and resource sales:

1. **Resource Extraction**: Corporations engage in resource extraction in partnership with governments, often operating in regions rife with corruption.

2. **Lobbying and Influence**: Corporations may use lobbying, political contributions, and other means to influence government policies and regulations in their favor.

3. **Supply Chains**: Supply chains for products like electronics and jewelry may be tainted by the use of conflict minerals or resources acquired through corruption.

4. **Secrecy Jurisdictions**: Some corporations use offshore tax havens and secrecy jurisdictions to hide profits and avoid taxation.

Consequences of Corruption and Exploitation: Human and Environmental Costs

The consequences of this nexus extend far beyond financial gains:

1. **Human Rights Abuses**: Exploitative practices can lead to human rights abuses, including forced labor and displacement.

2. **Environmental Degradation**: Irresponsible resource extraction can result in environmental destruction and the loss of biodiversity.

3. **Conflict and Instability**: Corruption and resource-driven conflicts can destabilize regions and lead to violence and suffering.

4. **Economic Stagnation**: Nations that fall prey to corruption and exploitation may experience economic stagnation and underdevelopment.

Efforts Towards Transparency and Accountability: A Path Forward

While the connection between corrupt leaders, global corporations, and resource sales is deeply entrenched, there are efforts to combat this nexus:

1. **Transparency Initiatives**: Organizations and governments are promoting transparency in resource contracts and payments to reduce corruption risks.

2. **Civil Society Vigilance**: Civil society organizations and activists play a crucial role in exposing corruption and advocating for accountability.

3. **Regulatory Reforms**: Some countries are implementing regulatory reforms to increase oversight of corporate practices and resource sales.

4. **International Cooperation**: Efforts at the international level seek to combat corruption and promote responsible resource management.

Conclusion: Breaking the Cycle of Exploitation

The connection between corrupt leaders, global corporations, and resource sales is a troubling reality that must be addressed. It is a cycle of exploitation that perpetuates poverty, inequality, and environmental degradation. Breaking this cycle requires concerted efforts at multiple levels - from transparent governance and accountable corporations to vigilant civil society and international cooperation. Only through these collective actions can we hope to dismantle the web of corruption and exploitation that ensnares nations and build a more equitable and sustainable future for all.

Implications for development, social equity, and global perceptions

Introduction: The Far-Reaching Impact

The intricate web of corruption, resource exploitation, and the actions of global corporations discussed in the previous chapter is not confined to isolated incidents; it has far-reaching implications that ripple through societies, economies, and international perceptions. In this chapter, we delve into the profound implications for development, social equity, and how the world views nations entangled in this complex nexus.

Development and the Resource Curse: A Paradox

Resource-rich nations often find themselves caught in the paradox of the resource curse, where an abundance of natural wealth becomes a curse rather than a blessing:

1. **Economic Dependency**: Heavy reliance on resource exports can lead to economic vulnerability, as fluctuations in global commodity prices directly impact a nation's fiscal health.

2. **Neglect of Other Sectors**: Overemphasis on resource extraction may lead to neglect of other sectors such as agriculture, manufacturing, and services, hindering economic diversification.

3. **Revenue Mismanagement**: Corrupt leaders may misappropriate resource revenues, diverting funds away from public services and development initiatives.

4. **Environmental Degradation**: Resource extraction often results in environmental damage, which can further impede sustainable development.

Social Equity and Inequality: Widening Disparities

The nexus of corruption and resource sales exacerbates social inequalities:

1. **Elite Capture**: Corrupt leaders and influential individuals often capture the benefits of resource sales, leaving ordinary citizens with little to no share in the wealth.

2. **Limited Access to Services**: Diversion of resources away from public services like healthcare and education disproportionately affects marginalized communities.

3. **Conflict and Displacement**: Resource-driven conflicts can displace vulnerable populations, worsening their living conditions.

4. **Gender Disparities**: Women and minority groups may be disproportionately affected by resource exploitation, facing discrimination and marginalization.

Global Perceptions and Reputation: The Stigma of Corruption

Nations embroiled in corruption and resource exploitation face reputational challenges:

1. **Loss of Trust**: Corruption erodes trust in governments and institutions, both domestically and internationally, damaging a nation's credibility.

2. **Investor Confidence**: Nations with a reputation for corruption may struggle to attract foreign investment, hindering economic growth.

3. **Aid and Assistance**: International donors and organizations may be hesitant to provide aid and assistance to nations with a history of corruption, affecting development programs.

4. **Stigmatization**: Nations may be stigmatized on the global stage, impacting their ability to engage in international diplomacy and trade.

Case Studies: Real-World Impact

To gain deeper insights into the implications of corruption, resource exploitation, and global corporate involvement, we examine case studies from diverse regions:

1. **Venezuela's Economic Collapse**: The rapid economic decline of Venezuela and the impact on

its population due to resource mismanagement and corruption.

2. **Angola's Resource Wealth**: The challenges Angola faces in leveraging its resource wealth for sustainable development and social equity.

3. **The Democratic Republic of Congo's Struggles**: The complex issues surrounding resource exploitation in the DRC and their implications for development and stability.

4. **Norway's Responsible Resource Management**: Norway's exemplary approach to resource management, which has led to equitable development and global respect.

Efforts for Mitigation and Reform: A Way Forward

Addressing the implications of corruption, resource exploitation, and global corporate involvement requires concerted efforts:

1. **Resource Revenue Management**: Implementing transparent mechanisms for managing resource revenues and directing them toward development.

2. **Accountability Measures**: Strengthening institutions and enforcing accountability measures to prevent corruption and resource misappropriation.

3. **Social Safety Nets**: Establishing social safety nets to protect vulnerable populations from the negative consequences of resource exploitation.

4. **Transparency Initiatives**: Participating in international transparency initiatives to promote responsible resource management.

Conclusion: Toward a More Equitable and Just World

The implications of corruption, resource exploitation, and global corporate actions are profound and pervasive. They challenge the very essence of development, equity, and a nation's global standing. Yet, as the world grapples with these complex issues, there remains hope for a brighter future. Through collective action, transparent governance, and a commitment to social justice, nations can break free from the shackles of corruption and exploitation. The path to a more equitable and just world begins with acknowledging the interconnectedness of our challenges and working together to overcome them, ensuring that development benefits all and leaving no one behind.

Chapter 9: Leaders and Legacy - Longevity and Power Consolidation

The prevalence of long-term leadership in African countries

Introduction: The Puzzle of Long-Term Leadership

Across the African continent, a notable phenomenon has persisted for decades - the prevalence of long-term leadership. In this chapter, we delve into the complex dynamics that allow leaders to consolidate power and extend their rule for extended periods. We explore the consequences of such leadership for nations and the enduring legacies they leave behind.

Understanding Long-Term Leadership: The Patterns and Characteristics

Before we dive into the exploration of long-term leadership, it is essential to understand its patterns and characteristics:

1. **Longevity in Office**: Long-term leaders remain in power for extended periods, often surpassing two or three decades.

2. **Power Consolidation**: They employ various strategies to consolidate their power, including changes to constitutions and electoral processes.

3. **Political Dominance**: Long-term leaders often dominate the political landscape, stifling opposition and suppressing dissent.

4. **Cults of Personality**: They cultivate strong cults of personality and engage in propaganda to maintain their popularity.

The Persistence of Long-Term Leadership: Factors and Mechanisms

The phenomenon of long-term leadership is sustained by a combination of factors and mechanisms:

1. **Weak Institutions**: Weak institutional checks and balances create opportunities for leaders to extend their rule.

2. **Election Manipulation**: Manipulation of elections, voter suppression, and tampering with the electoral process can ensure continued victories.

3. **Resource Control**: Control over valuable resources, such as oil or minerals, provides leaders with the means to maintain loyalty.

4. **Repression**: The use of repression, including the silencing of opposition and media censorship, helps leaders retain power.

Case Studies: African Leaders and Their Legacies

To gain deeper insights into the phenomenon of long-term leadership and its consequences, we examine case studies from diverse African nations:

1. **Robert Mugabe - Zimbabwe's Longest-Serving Leader**: The reign of Robert Mugabe, his land reforms, and their impact on Zimbabwe's economy and politics.

2. **Yoweri Museveni - Uganda's Stalwart**: Yoweri Museveni's extended rule in Uganda and its effects on the nation's political landscape.

3. **Paul Biya - Cameroon's Silent Dominator**: Paul Biya's enduring leadership in Cameroon and the challenges faced by the country.

4. **Teodoro Obiang Nguema Mbasogo - Equatorial Guinea's Strongman**: The rule of Teodoro Obiang Nguema Mbasogo and its implications for the nation's resources and political stability.

5. **Isaias Afwerki - Eritrea's Enigmatic Leader**: The leadership of Isaias Afwerki in Eritrea and the nation's isolation on the global stage.

Consequences of Long-Term Leadership: A Double-Edged Sword

Long-term leadership brings both positive and negative consequences for nations:

1. **Stability**: Some long-term leaders have provided stability and economic growth during their tenures.

2. **Repression**: Repression of dissent and opposition can lead to human rights abuses and political instability.

3. **Economic Mismanagement**: Prolonged rule may result in economic mismanagement and a lack of innovation.

4. **Erosion of Institutions**: Institutions may be eroded, weakening democratic principles and checks on power.

Efforts Toward Change: Challenges and Resistance

Efforts to challenge long-term leadership face significant obstacles:

1. **Repression**: Leaders often respond to challenges with repression, making opposition difficult.

2. **Weak Opposition**: A weak and fragmented opposition can struggle to mount a credible challenge.

3. **International Pressure**: International pressure may be limited due to geopolitical considerations.

4. **Economic Dependence**: Economic dependence on the leader's regime may hinder resistance efforts.

Legacy and Transition: The Dilemma of Succession

The issue of succession looms large in long-term leadership:

1. **Succession Planning**: Leaders may groom family members or loyalists for succession, raising concerns of dynastic rule.

2. **Transition Challenges**: The transition of power, whether through elections or other means, can be fraught with challenges and uncertainties.

3. **Legacy**: Long-term leaders leave a lasting legacy, for better or worse, that shapes the nation's future.

Conclusion: The Quest for Renewal and Accountability

The prevalence of long-term leadership in African countries is a complex and enduring phenomenon with both positive and negative consequences. It challenges the principles of democracy and accountability, yet it also offers stability in some cases. As nations grapple with this puzzle, the quest for renewal, democratic governance, and leadership accountability remains a critical journey. The legacies of long-term leaders will continue to shape the future of African countries, and the choices made by both leaders and citizens will determine the path forward. In this evolving landscape, the balance between stability and change is a delicate one, but it is a balance that must be struck to ensure the prosperity and well-being of nations and their citizens.

Analysis of factors contributing to extended leadership tenures

Introduction: Unlocking the Enigma of Extended Leadership

The phenomenon of leaders serving extended tenures in political office is a complex puzzle that has confounded scholars, policymakers, and citizens alike. In this chapter, we embark on a comprehensive analysis of the multifaceted factors that contribute to leaders staying in power for prolonged periods, with a focus on the African context. By dissecting these factors, we aim to shed light on the enigma of extended leadership tenures.

Factors at the Heart of Extended Leadership

Before we delve into the analysis, it is crucial to identify and define the primary factors that underpin extended leadership tenures:

1. **Political Manipulation**: The use of political maneuvers, electoral tactics, and constitutional changes to manipulate the political landscape in favor of the incumbent.

2. **Economic Leverage**: Control over valuable economic resources, such as oil, minerals, or a dominant industry, that provides the leader with the means to secure loyalty and finance their campaigns.

3. **Repression and Control**: The use of force, repression of opposition, and control of state institutions to stifle dissent and opposition.

4. **Popularity and Charisma**: A leader's ability to cultivate a cult of personality, garner popular support, and maintain charisma that resonates with the electorate.

Political Manipulation: The Art of Staying in Power

Political manipulation is a cornerstone of extended leadership tenures:

1. **Constitutional Changes**: Leaders may amend constitutions to remove term limits or expand their powers, ensuring their continued rule.

2. **Electoral Tactics**: Manipulation of electoral processes, voter suppression, and gerrymandering can guarantee election victories.

3. **Opposition Fragmentation**: Efforts to divide and weaken the opposition through co-optation or coercion.

4. **Electioneering**: Use of state resources for campaigning, control of the media, and intimidation of political opponents.

Economic Leverage: The Power of Wealth

Economic leverage plays a pivotal role in sustaining extended leadership:

1. **Resource Control**: Leaders who control valuable resources can use them to secure loyalty, finance their campaigns, and fund patronage networks.

2. **Corruption and Wealth Accumulation**: The accumulation of personal wealth through corrupt practices can provide leaders with financial security and political clout.

3. **Elite Patronage**: Dispensing economic benefits to a select group of loyal elites helps maintain their support.

Repression and Control: The Iron Fist

Repression and control are tools used to suppress dissent and opposition:

1. **Media Censorship**: Control of the media landscape to limit criticism and dissenting voices.

2. **Security Apparatus**: A strong security apparatus, including a loyal military and intelligence agencies, can quash opposition.

3. **Harassment and Imprisonment**: The use of harassment, intimidation, and imprisonment of political opponents and activists.

Popularity and Charisma: The Personal Connection

The personal qualities of a leader can play a significant role in extended leadership tenures:

1. **Cult of Personality**: Cultivating an image of the leader as a national hero or savior can engender loyalty and popularity.

2. **Charismatic Appeal**: The ability to connect with the electorate on an emotional level and inspire trust and support.

3. **Effective Communication**: Leaders who communicate effectively and resonate with the concerns of the population are often more successful in staying in power.

Case Studies: African Leaders and Extended Tenures

To illustrate the interplay of these factors, we examine case studies of African leaders known for their extended tenures:

1. **Yoweri Museveni - Uganda's Political Chameleon**: The strategies employed by Yoweri

Museveni to maintain power in Uganda for over three decades.

2. **Omar al-Bashir - Sudan's Authoritarian Legacy**: The reign of Omar al-Bashir and how he managed to stay in power despite international pressure.

3. **Paul Biya - Cameroon's Silent Dominator**: Paul Biya's extended rule in Cameroon and his ability to suppress opposition.

4. **Robert Mugabe - Zimbabwe's Fallen Hero**: Robert Mugabe's rise to power and the factors that allowed him to maintain control for nearly four decades.

Consequences of Extended Leadership: A Mixed Bag

Extended leadership tenures have both positive and negative consequences:

1. **Stability**: Extended leadership can provide stability and continuity in governance, which is valued in some contexts.

2. **Repression and Stagnation**: Repression of dissent and a lack of innovation can lead to political stagnation and economic mismanagement.

3. **Erosion of Democracy**: Extended leadership can erode democratic principles and weaken institutions designed to provide checks and balances.

4. **Legacy**: Leaders who serve extended tenures leave a lasting legacy that shapes the nation's future, for better or worse.

Challenges to Change: Breaking the Cycle

Efforts to challenge extended leadership tenures face significant challenges:

1. **Repression**: Leaders often respond to challenges with repression, making it difficult for opposition movements to gain traction.

2. **Weak Opposition**: Fragmented and weak opposition movements may struggle to mount credible challenges.

3. **International Influence**: International actors may be limited in their ability to influence leadership change, especially in resource-rich nations.

4. **Economic Dependency**: Economic dependency on the leader's regime can hinder resistance efforts.

Conclusion: The Quest for Renewal and Accountability

The analysis of factors contributing to extended leadership tenures reveals a complex interplay of political, economic, and social dynamics. While some leaders use manipulation and control to stay in power, others may genuinely enjoy popular support. The consequences of extended leadership are a mixed bag, with both positive stability and negative repression and stagnation. The quest for renewal, accountability, and democratic governance continues to be a crucial journey for nations seeking to balance the need for stability with the imperative of change. The choices made by leaders, citizens, and the international community will ultimately determine the path forward in this complex landscape of extended leadership.

The consequences of entrenched leadership on governance and development

Introduction: The Impact of Long-Term Leadership

Entrenched leadership, characterized by leaders who stay in power for extended periods, has a profound impact on governance and development. In this chapter, we delve into the consequences of such leadership on the political landscape, governance structures, and the overall development trajectory of nations, with a particular focus on the African context. By examining these consequences, we aim to provide a comprehensive understanding of the challenges and opportunities presented by entrenched leadership.

Entrenched Leadership: Defining the Phenomenon

Before we analyze the consequences, it is essential to define entrenched leadership and its key characteristics:

1. **Extended Tenure**: Leaders who remain in power for multiple terms, often exceeding two decades.

2. **Power Consolidation**: Strategies employed to maintain and consolidate power, such as constitutional changes or electoral manipulation.

3. **Political Dominance**: Leaders who dominate the political landscape, often stifling opposition and dissent.

4. **Legacy Building**: Cultivation of a strong legacy and cult of personality, which can influence public perception and support.

Consequences for Governance: The Power Dilemma

Entrenched leadership has far-reaching consequences for governance:

1. **Erosion of Democratic Norms**: Long-term leaders may erode democratic norms and institutions, leading to a concentration of power.

2. **Weakened Institutions**: Key institutions, including the judiciary and legislature, may be

weakened or co-opted, reducing their ability to provide checks and balances.

3. **Limited Accountability**: Leaders may face limited accountability for their actions, including corruption or human rights abuses.

4. **Impediments to Political Renewal**: The absence of leadership turnover can impede political renewal and the emergence of new ideas and perspectives.

Economic Implications: Balancing Stability and Growth

The economic consequences of entrenched leadership are complex:

1. **Stability vs. Stagnation**: Extended leadership can provide stability, which is valued by investors and can foster economic growth. However, it can also lead to political and economic stagnation if leaders become complacent.

2. **Resource Mismanagement**: Leaders who control valuable resources may mismanage them, leading to economic instability and inequality.

3. **Corruption and Patronage**: Extended tenures may be associated with corruption and patronage networks that divert resources away from development.

4. **Dependency on Key Industries**: Economic strategies may become overly dependent on a

single industry or sector, making nations vulnerable to global economic fluctuations.

Social and Human Development: Winners and Losers

The consequences of entrenched leadership extend to social and human development:

1. **Winner-Takes-All**: Resource allocation and development projects may favor regions or groups aligned with the leader, leaving marginalized communities behind.

2. **Social Services and Infrastructure**: Investment in essential services like healthcare, education, and infrastructure may suffer due to resource diversion or neglect.

3. **Brain Drain**: The lack of opportunities and political freedom can lead to a brain drain, where skilled professionals emigrate in search of better prospects.

4. **Social Cohesion**: Prolonged leadership can strain social cohesion, leading to divisions and tensions within societies.

Case Studies: African Nations and Entrenched Leadership

To illustrate the consequences of entrenched leadership, we examine case studies from African nations:

1. **Museveni's Uganda**: The impact of Yoweri Museveni's extended rule on Uganda's political landscape and development trajectory.

Yoweri Kaguta Museveni is one of the longest-serving leaders in Africa, having been in power in Uganda since January 29, 1986. His extended rule has had profound consequences on Uganda's political landscape and its development trajectory. Here's an overview of the key aspects of Museveni's rule and their impact:

1. Longevity in Office: Museveni's uninterrupted tenure of nearly four decades has resulted in a significant concentration of power. He has held the presidency through multiple elections, with some observers arguing that his rule has stifled the country's democratic processes.

Impact:

- **Erosion of Democratic Norms:** Over time, Museveni's rule has seen the erosion of democratic norms and practices in Uganda. Critics argue that elections have become less competitive, with allegations of electoral manipulation and suppression of political opposition.

- **Limited Political Renewal:** The extended tenure of Museveni has limited political renewal in Uganda. New political voices and parties face challenges in gaining a foothold in the political landscape.

2. Political Dominance: Museveni's rule has been marked by a strong political dominance, with his party, the National Resistance Movement (NRM), maintaining a firm grip on power.

Impact:

- **Weakened Opposition:** The NRM's political dominance has often left the opposition fragmented and weakened, making it challenging for them to mount credible challenges in elections.

- **Concentration of Power:** Museveni's presidency has been characterized by a centralization of power, which has implications for checks and balances within the political system.

3. Economic Development: Museveni's rule has seen Uganda experience periods of economic growth, particularly in the 1990s and 2000s. His government has implemented economic reforms, attracted foreign investment, and promoted infrastructure development.

Impact:

- **Economic Growth:** Uganda has achieved periods of economic growth under Museveni's leadership, which has contributed to improved living standards for some segments of the population.

- **Challenges of Inclusivity:** However, economic growth has not always been inclusive, with disparities between urban and rural areas, as well as different regions of the country.

4. Challenges and Criticisms: Museveni's extended rule has faced criticism and challenges.

Impact:

- **Human Rights Concerns:** His government has faced allegations of human rights abuses, including restrictions on freedom of the press and political repression.

- **Youth Unemployment:** Despite economic growth, Uganda still grapples with high levels of youth unemployment, which has fueled discontent among the youth population.

5. Legacy and Succession: Museveni's extended rule has raised questions about succession planning.

Impact:

- **Uncertainty:** Uncertainty regarding succession and the potential for a dynastic transfer of power to his son has generated concern among Ugandans and the international community.

In summary, Yoweri Museveni's extended rule in Uganda has had a multifaceted impact. While there have been periods of economic growth and stability, there are also concerns about the erosion of democratic norms, political dominance, and human rights abuses. The legacy of his leadership and the path Uganda takes in the post-Museveni era will continue to shape the country's political landscape and development trajectory.

2. **Zimbabwe's Mugabe Era**: The legacy of Robert Mugabe's lengthy presidency and its consequences for governance, the economy, and human development.

Robert Mugabe's lengthy presidency in Zimbabwe, spanning nearly four decades from 1980 to 2017, left a significant and complex legacy that had profound consequences for governance, the economy, and human development. Here's an exploration of the key aspects of Mugabe's era and its impact:

1. Authoritarian Rule: Mugabe's presidency was marked by an increasingly authoritarian style of governance, characterized by political repression and the stifling of dissent.

Impact:

- **Erosion of Democracy:** Under Mugabe's rule, Zimbabwe's democratic institutions weakened, and the country experienced a decline in political freedoms and electoral integrity.

- **Human Rights Abuses:** There were numerous allegations of human rights abuses, including political violence, forced evictions, and intimidation of political opponents.

2. Land Reforms: One of the most contentious policies of Mugabe's era was the fast-track land reform program initiated in the early 2000s, which led to the seizure of white-owned commercial farms.

Impact:

- **Economic Consequences:** The land reforms disrupted agricultural production and contributed to a significant economic downturn, marked by hyperinflation and unemployment.

- **Humanitarian Crisis:** The land seizures triggered a humanitarian crisis, with displacement of farm workers and food shortages affecting ordinary Zimbabweans.

3. Economic Mismanagement: Mugabe's tenure saw a period of economic mismanagement, marked by hyperinflation, currency instability, and a collapsing economy.

Impact:

- **Economic Collapse:** Zimbabwe experienced one of the worst economic collapses in modern history, with hyperinflation reaching astronomical levels, rendering the Zimbabwean dollar virtually worthless.

- **Mass Emigration:** The economic hardships drove mass emigration, with Zimbabweans seeking better opportunities abroad, leading to a brain drain.

4. Legacy of Political Stability: In contrast to some African countries, Zimbabwe experienced relative political stability under Mugabe's rule, with no major civil wars or coups.

Impact:

- **Stability Amidst Challenges:** While the country faced severe economic and political challenges, it did not descend into widespread violence or civil war, maintaining a degree of political stability.

5. Impact on Human Development: Mugabe's era had mixed consequences for human development indicators.

Impact:

- **Education:** Zimbabwe's education system, once considered one of the best in Africa, experienced declines in funding and quality during Mugabe's tenure.

- **Healthcare:** The healthcare system faced challenges, including shortages of medicines and healthcare professionals.

6. Political Succession and Ouster: The end of Mugabe's presidency in 2017 marked a tumultuous period of political transition.

Impact:

- **End of an Era:** Mugabe's ouster marked the end of an era in Zimbabwean politics, leading to hopes for political and economic reforms under new leadership.

In summary, Robert Mugabe's lengthy presidency in Zimbabwe left a complex legacy characterized by authoritarian rule, economic mismanagement, and a controversial land reform program. While the country experienced relative political stability, it also faced economic collapse and challenges to human development. Mugabe's legacy continues to shape Zimbabwe's political and economic landscape, as the country strives to overcome the challenges and move toward a more stable and prosperous future.

3. **Biya's Cameroon:** The enduring leadership of Paul Biya in Cameroon and its effects on political stability and economic growth.

Paul Biya's long-lasting leadership in Cameroon, which began in 1982 and continues to this day, has had a significant impact on the country's political stability and economic growth. Here's an analysis of the key aspects of Biya's rule and their implications:

1. Longevity in Office: Paul Biya's rule in Cameroon has been characterized by uninterrupted leadership spanning several decades, making him one of Africa's longest-serving leaders.

Impact:

- **Political Stability:** Biya's long tenure has contributed to political stability in Cameroon compared to some African countries that have experienced coups or civil wars.

- **Limited Political Renewal:** The extended rule has limited political renewal and the emergence of new leaders, potentially hindering fresh perspectives and ideas.

2. Political Dominance: Biya's party, the Cameroon People's Democratic Movement (CPDM), has maintained a dominant position in Cameroonian politics.

Impact:

- **Weak Opposition:** The CPDM's political dominance has often left the opposition fragmented and struggling to mount credible challenges in elections.

- **Centralization of Power:** Biya's presidency has been marked by a centralization of power, which has implications for checks and balances within the political system.

3. Economic Development: Under Biya's leadership, Cameroon has experienced periods of economic growth and development.

Impact:

- **Economic Stability:** Biya's government has managed to maintain relative economic stability, attracting foreign investment and promoting infrastructure development.

- **Resource Management Challenges:** However, there have been concerns about resource management, particularly in regions with valuable resources such as oil and minerals.

4. Challenges and Criticisms: Biya's rule has faced criticisms and challenges.

Impact:

- **Human Rights Concerns:** There have been allegations of human rights abuses and political repression, including crackdowns on political opponents.

- **Regional Conflicts:** Biya's government has grappled with regional conflicts, particularly in the Anglophone regions, which have had implications for stability.

5. Legacy and Succession: Questions about succession planning and the future of leadership in Cameroon have emerged due to Biya's advanced age.

Impact:

- **Uncertainty:** Uncertainty regarding succession has generated concerns about the country's political future and the potential for instability during a transition.

6. Regional Dynamics: Cameroon's role in regional politics, particularly in the Central African region, has been influenced by Biya's leadership.

Impact:

- **Regional Mediator:** Cameroon has played a role as a mediator in regional conflicts and has been involved in peacekeeping efforts, contributing to regional stability.

In summary, Paul Biya's enduring leadership in Cameroon has had a multifaceted impact. While it has provided relative political stability and periods of economic growth, it has also faced criticisms regarding political repression and human rights abuses. The future of leadership in Cameroon, especially considering Biya's advanced age, remains a significant concern as the nation navigates its political and economic challenges.

4. **Obiang's Equatorial Guinea:** Teodoro Obiang Nguema Mbasogo's rule in Equatorial Guinea and its implications for resource management and governance.

Teodoro Obiang Nguema Mbasogo's lengthy rule in Equatorial Guinea, which began in 1979, has had profound implications for resource management and governance in the country. Here's an exploration of key aspects of Obiang's rule and their impact:

1. Extended Tenure: Obiang's rule in Equatorial Guinea has spanned several decades, making him one of Africa's longest-serving leaders.

Impact:

- **Political Stability:** His extended tenure has provided a degree of political stability, with no major civil wars or coups during his rule.

- **Limited Political Pluralism:** The political landscape has been characterized by limited political pluralism, with the ruling Democratic Party of Equatorial Guinea (PDGE) maintaining dominance.

2. Resource Wealth: Equatorial Guinea is rich in oil and gas resources, and Obiang's rule has coincided with significant oil discoveries and production.

Impact:

- **Resource Mismanagement:** Despite substantial oil wealth, Equatorial Guinea has faced challenges related to resource mismanagement, corruption, and lack of transparency.

- **Limited Benefits for Citizens:** The majority of the population has not seen significant improvements in living standards, and poverty persists, despite the country's oil wealth.

3. Governance and Human Rights: Obiang's regime has faced allegations of human rights abuses and lack of political freedoms.

Impact:

- **Authoritarian Rule:** Equatorial Guinea has been characterized by authoritarian rule, with restrictions on political opposition and dissent.

- **Limited Accountability:** There has been limited accountability for allegations of corruption and human rights abuses within the government.

4. Economic Disparities: While the country has experienced economic growth due to oil revenues, disparities between the ruling elite and the general population have persisted.

Impact:

- **Economic Inequality:** The benefits of economic growth have disproportionately favored the ruling elite, leaving the majority of the population in poverty.

- **Lack of Diversification:** The heavy reliance on oil and gas has left the economy vulnerable to fluctuations in global oil prices.

5. Regional and International Relations: Equatorial Guinea's role in regional and international politics has been influenced by Obiang's leadership.

Impact:

- **International Scrutiny:** The country has faced scrutiny from international organizations and human rights groups due to governance and human rights concerns.

- **Regional Relations:** Equatorial Guinea's relations with neighboring countries have varied, with occasional tensions and diplomatic disputes.

6. Succession and Uncertainty: Questions about succession and the future leadership of Equatorial Guinea have emerged due to Obiang's advanced age.

Impact:

- **Uncertainty:** The lack of a clear succession plan has generated uncertainty about the country's political future and potential instability during a transition.

In summary, Teodoro Obiang Nguema Mbasogo's lengthy rule in Equatorial Guinea has had significant implications for resource management, governance, and human rights. While the country has benefited from oil wealth, challenges related to corruption, economic disparities, and lack of political freedoms have persisted. The future of leadership in Equatorial Guinea remains uncertain, and the country continues to grapple with complex political and economic issues.

Challenges to Change: Breaking the Cycle

Efforts to challenge entrenched leadership face significant obstacles:

1. **Repression**: Leaders often respond to challenges with repression, making it difficult for opposition movements to gain traction.

2. **Weak Opposition**: Fragmented and weak opposition movements may struggle to mount credible challenges.
3. **International Influence**: International actors may be limited in their ability to influence leadership change, especially in resource-rich nations.

4. **Economic Dependency**: Economic dependency on the leader's regime can hinder resistance efforts.

Conclusion: Balancing Stability and Renewal

The consequences of entrenched leadership on governance and development are a complex interplay of stability, stagnation, and inequity. While long-term leaders may provide stability, they can also erode democratic norms, weaken institutions, and mismanage resources. The challenge lies in striking a balance between stability and renewal, ensuring that leaders are held accountable, institutions are strengthened, and development benefits all segments of society. The choices made by leaders, citizens, and the international community will ultimately determine the path forward in navigating the complex terrain of entrenched leadership.

Chapter 10: Aspirations Amidst Adversity - Grassroots Movements and Progress

Showcasing the resilience and agency of African communities

Introduction: The Resilience of African Communities

In the face of the numerous challenges highlighted in previous chapters, African communities have consistently demonstrated remarkable resilience and agency. This chapter delves into the inspiring stories of grassroots movements and initiatives that have emerged across the continent. These stories showcase the determination of ordinary Africans to overcome adversity and drive progress in various spheres of life.

The Resilience of African Communities

African communities have a long history of resilience, dating back to pre-colonial times. This section explores the historical context of community resilience, highlighting traditional practices and values that have contributed to the ability to adapt and thrive.

Traditional Knowledge and Sustainability

African communities have a wealth of traditional knowledge that has sustained them for generations. This knowledge encompasses various aspects of life, from agriculture to medicine. We examine how this traditional wisdom is being preserved and integrated into modern sustainable practices.

Agricultural Innovations and Food Security

Food security remains a critical concern in many African countries. This section explores grassroots initiatives focused on agricultural innovations, such as urban farming and sustainable farming techniques, that are helping communities achieve greater food security.

Healthcare Initiatives and Access to Medical Services

Access to healthcare is a fundamental human right, yet it remains a challenge for many in Africa. We discuss how community-based healthcare initiatives, including mobile clinics and community health workers, are bridging the gap and improving healthcare access.

Education for All: Bridging the Knowledge Divide

Education is a powerful tool for empowerment and progress. In this section, we explore grassroots efforts to ensure education reaches all segments of society, including initiatives to build schools in remote areas and promote girls' education.

Environmental Conservation and Sustainable Development

African communities are at the forefront of environmental conservation efforts. We delve into the work of local conservationists and community-led initiatives aimed at protecting natural resources and promoting sustainable development.

Women's Empowerment and Gender Equality

Gender equality remains a pressing issue in many African societies. This section highlights grassroots movements that are championing women's rights, promoting gender equality, and challenging harmful traditional practices.

Youth-Led Initiatives and Social Change

African youth are taking charge of their futures. We explore youth-led movements that are advocating for social change, addressing issues such as unemployment, political reform, and climate change.

Conflict Resolution and Peacebuilding

Many African communities have been affected by conflict and violence. We discuss grassroots peacebuilding efforts that bring together diverse community members to heal wounds and build peace.

Case Studies: Inspirational Stories of Resilience

Throughout the chapter, we feature case studies from various African countries, showcasing the individuals and communities behind these grassroots movements. These stories provide real-world examples of the remarkable achievements and resilience of African communities.

Challenges and Opportunities

While grassroots movements have made significant strides, they also face challenges, including limited resources and recognition. We examine these challenges and explore opportunities for greater support and collaboration.

Conclusion: A Brighter Future Through Grassroots Action

In closing, we reflect on the enduring spirit of African communities and the potential for grassroots movements to drive positive change. The stories shared in this chapter offer hope and inspiration, highlighting that even in the face of adversity, progress is possible when communities come together with determination and agency. Africa's future is shaped not only by its challenges but also by the aspirations and actions of its people.

Empowerment through grassroots initiatives, civil society, and activism

Introduction: The Power of Grassroots Empowerment

In a world often characterized by complex challenges and inequalities, grassroots initiatives, civil society organizations, and activism have emerged as powerful tools for empowerment. This chapter explores the various ways in which individuals and communities harness their agency to effect positive change, advance social justice, and empower themselves and others.

Empowerment at the Grassroots: An Overview

Grassroots empowerment refers to the process by which individuals, often at the community level, take control of their lives and work collectively to address their needs and aspirations. This section provides an overview of the concept of grassroots empowerment and its significance in fostering inclusive development.

The Role of Civil Society: Catalysts of Change

Civil society organizations play a vital role in advocating for social justice, human rights, and sustainable development. We delve into the diverse functions of civil society, from service delivery to policy advocacy, and highlight their contributions to empowerment.

Activism as a Force for Change

Activism is a dynamic and influential force that can challenge the status quo and drive societal transformation. We explore the various forms of activism, from street protests to online advocacy, and discuss how activists mobilize for change.

The Intersection of Grassroots and Technology

The digital age has revolutionized grassroots empowerment. We examine how technology, including social media and mobile apps, has amplified the voices of grassroots movements and facilitated global solidarity.

Gender Equality and Women's Empowerment

Gender equality is central to empowerment. We explore how grassroots initiatives and women's movements are dismantling patriarchal structures, advocating for women's rights, and promoting gender equality.

Youth-Led Movements: A New Wave of Empowerment

The youth are at the forefront of contemporary social and political movements. We delve into youth-led initiatives that address issues such as climate change, education access, and political reform.

Environmental Activism and Sustainability

Environmental challenges threaten the well-being of communities worldwide. Grassroots environmental activism is vital for conservation efforts, climate action, and the protection of natural resources.

Empowering Marginalized Communities

Marginalized communities often face systemic barriers. We explore initiatives that empower marginalized groups, including indigenous communities, refugees, and the LGBTQ+ community.

Education for Empowerment

Education is a powerful tool for empowerment. We discuss initiatives that prioritize access to quality education, adult literacy programs, and educational advocacy as pathways to empowerment.

Healthcare Access and Empowerment

Access to healthcare is a fundamental human right. We examine grassroots healthcare initiatives, community health workers, and healthcare advocacy efforts that empower individuals to take charge of their health.

Case Studies in Empowerment

Throughout the chapter, we feature case studies from different regions of the world, showcasing grassroots initiatives, civil society organizations, and activists making a difference. These real-life examples demonstrate the impact of grassroots empowerment.

Challenges and Future Prospects

Grassroots empowerment faces challenges, including resource constraints, political repression, and the need for sustained support. We discuss these challenges and outline potential strategies for overcoming them.

Conclusion: The Ongoing Journey of Empowerment

In closing, we reflect on the enduring journey of empowerment through grassroots initiatives, civil society, and activism. Empowerment is not a destination but an ongoing process of striving for justice, equality, and human dignity. It is a testament to the resilience and agency of individuals and communities working together to create a more equitable and empowered world.

Success stories and lessons from local efforts to effect change

Introduction: The Power of Local Initiatives

At the heart of every significant social and societal transformation lie the efforts of local communities, grassroots organizations, and individuals who have dedicated themselves to bringing about positive change. This chapter delves into a multitude of success stories and the invaluable lessons learned from local endeavors that have left an indelible mark on the world. Through these stories, we gain insight into the profound impact that locally driven change can have on addressing global challenges.

The Local Heroes: Driving Change from Within

Local efforts often epitomize the spirit of resilience, determination, and agency. We introduce the concept of local heroes and the role they play in initiating and leading transformative initiatives within their communities.

The Power of Community Engagement

Community engagement is the bedrock of local initiatives. We explore how communities come together to identify challenges, set priorities, and collaboratively design solutions that resonate with their unique contexts.

Sustainable Development at the Local Level

Sustainable development is not just a global goal; it's a tangible reality in countless localities. We delve into examples of local sustainable development initiatives that prioritize economic growth, environmental stewardship, and social equity.

Education for All: Local Innovations in Learning

Education is a powerful catalyst for change, and local initiatives are at the forefront of efforts to expand access to quality education. We highlight local innovations in learning, from community-based schools to digital learning platforms.

Environmental Stewardship and Conservation

Local communities are often the custodians of natural resources. We explore how grassroots conservation efforts, reforestation projects, and sustainable agriculture practices are making a tangible impact on the environment.

Healthcare Access and Local Solutions

Access to healthcare is a fundamental right, and local healthcare initiatives bridge the gap between communities and essential medical services. We discuss models of community healthcare, telemedicine, and healthcare advocacy.

Empowering Women and Promoting Gender Equality

Empowering women and advancing gender equality are central to sustainable development. We feature stories of local initiatives that challenge gender norms, promote women's rights, and create pathways to equality.

Youth-Led Movements: Catalysts for Change

Youth-led movements have the power to challenge the status quo and ignite social change. We examine youth-led initiatives addressing issues such as climate action, political reform, and social justice.

Technology and Innovation: A Local Lens

Technology has revolutionized local development efforts. We explore how local communities are leveraging technology for purposes such as e-governance, connectivity, and economic development.

Resilience in the Face of Adversity

Communities often face adversity, from natural disasters to conflict. We highlight stories of resilience, showcasing how communities rebuild and adapt in the aftermath of challenges.

Case Studies in Local Change

Throughout the chapter, we present a diverse range of case studies from various regions of the world, offering insights into the strategies, successes, and challenges faced by local initiatives.

Lessons Learned and Best Practices

Drawing from the experiences of local initiatives, we distill key lessons and best practices for effecting positive change at the grassroots level. These insights provide guidance for future endeavors.

Challenges and the Road Ahead

Local initiatives are not without challenges, including resource limitations, policy constraints, and the need for sustained support. We discuss these challenges and explore strategies for addressing them.

Conclusion: The Enduring Impact of Local Efforts

In conclusion, we reflect on the enduring impact of local efforts to effect change. These stories illustrate the transformative potential that resides within communities and individuals. They remind us that change is not solely the purview of global institutions but a collective endeavor that begins at the local level. As we celebrate the successes and lessons from local initiatives, we are inspired to continue supporting and nurturing the changemakers who are shaping a better world, one community at a time.

Chapter 11: Visioning Tomorrow - Shaping Africa's Future

The role of education, innovation, and technology in overcoming challenges

Introduction: The Imperative of Shaping Africa's Future

As we contemplate Africa's future, we are faced with a dual reality - the continent's abundant potential and the persistent challenges that have hindered its progress. This chapter explores the critical role that education, innovation, and technology play in charting a path forward, enabling Africa to harness its potential and overcome the obstacles that have held it back for too long.

The Power of Education: A Foundation for Transformation

Education is the cornerstone of progress. We delve into the transformative potential of education, from early childhood development to higher education, in equipping Africans with the knowledge and skills needed to build a brighter future.

Quality Education for All: The Quest for Inclusivity

Inclusivity in education is essential for equitable development. We explore strategies and initiatives that aim to ensure that education reaches all segments of society, including marginalized groups and underserved regions.

Innovation Ecosystems: Fostering Creativity and Entrepreneurship

Innovation is a driver of economic growth and societal change. We examine the development of innovation ecosystems, startup hubs, and entrepreneurship initiatives that are fueling innovation across Africa.

The Role of Technology: Connectivity and Access

Technology has the potential to bridge divides and catalyze development. We discuss efforts to expand digital connectivity, digital literacy, and access to technology in rural and remote areas.

Transformative Impact of Artificial Intelligence and Data Science

Artificial Intelligence (AI) and data science are poised to revolutionize various sectors. We explore how African countries are leveraging AI and data analytics for purposes such as healthcare, agriculture, and disaster management.

Green Technologies and Sustainable Practices

Sustainability is a global imperative. We highlight green technologies, renewable energy projects, and sustainable agricultural practices that promote environmental stewardship and economic growth.

Empowering Youth: Preparing the Next Generation of Leaders

Youth represent Africa's greatest asset. We discuss programs that empower youth through education, mentorship, and leadership development, preparing them to take on leadership roles in various sectors.

Women in STEM: Breaking Barriers and Driving Innovation

Gender equality in STEM fields is crucial for innovation. We showcase initiatives that encourage women and girls to pursue STEM careers, challenging gender stereotypes and fostering diversity.

Higher Education and Research Excellence

Higher education institutions are hubs of knowledge creation. We explore the growth of research excellence, academic partnerships, and centers of excellence that contribute to Africa's development.

Healthcare Innovations: Improving Access and Quality

Access to quality healthcare remains a challenge in many African countries. We discuss healthcare innovations, telemedicine, and digital health solutions that enhance healthcare access and delivery.

Smart Cities and Urban Planning

Urbanization is reshaping Africa. We look at smart city initiatives, urban planning, and sustainable infrastructure development that accommodate rapid urban growth.

Harnessing Agriculture and Agribusiness

Agriculture is the backbone of many African economies. We examine innovations in agriculture, agribusiness, and value chain development that drive economic growth and food security.

Case Studies in Transformation

Throughout the chapter, we present case studies from different African countries, illustrating how education, innovation, and technology are driving transformative change.

Challenges and the Way Forward

While progress is evident, challenges persist. We discuss the obstacles facing education, innovation, and technology in Africa and propose strategies for overcoming them.

Conclusion: A Vision of Africa's Bright Future

In closing, we envision a future where Africa's potential is fully realized through education, innovation, and technology. These transformative forces empower individuals and communities to address challenges, drive economic growth, and shape Africa's destiny. Africa's bright future is not a distant dream but an attainable vision, and it is within our collective power to make it a reality.

Strategies for fostering inclusive growth, equitable development, and good governance

Introduction: The Imperative of Inclusivity and Good Governance

Inclusivity, equitable development, and good governance are fundamental pillars of sustainable progress. This chapter explores a range of strategies that African nations can employ to foster inclusive growth, ensure equitable development, and establish good governance practices. These strategies aim to address historical disparities, promote social cohesion, and create a conducive environment for sustainable development.

1. Inclusive Economic Policies

Inclusivity in economic policies is crucial for reducing income inequality and fostering equitable development. We delve into strategies such as progressive taxation, targeted social spending, and pro-poor economic policies that prioritize the well-being of vulnerable populations.

2. Strengthening Education Systems

Education is the key to breaking cycles of poverty and inequality. We explore strategies to strengthen education systems, including investments in teacher training, curriculum reform, and efforts to ensure access to quality education for all.

3. Empowering Women and Girls

Gender equality is a cornerstone of inclusive development. We discuss strategies to empower women and girls through initiatives such as gender-sensitive laws, economic opportunities, and healthcare access, breaking down barriers to their full participation in society.

4. Rural Development and Agriculture

Rural areas often face disparities in development. We examine strategies to promote rural development, including investments in agricultural productivity, infrastructure, and access to markets, ensuring that rural communities share in the benefits of growth.

5. Healthcare Access and Universal Health Coverage

Access to healthcare is a fundamental right. We discuss strategies to improve healthcare access, including the expansion of healthcare infrastructure, community health programs, and efforts to achieve universal health coverage.

6. Infrastructure Development

Infrastructure is a catalyst for economic growth. We explore strategies for infrastructure development, including investments in transportation, energy, and telecommunications that connect regions and promote economic activity.

7. Social Safety Nets

Social safety nets are critical for protecting vulnerable populations. We examine strategies to establish and expand social safety nets, providing a buffer against shocks and promoting social cohesion.

8. Promoting Entrepreneurship and Innovation

Entrepreneurship and innovation drive economic growth. We discuss strategies to foster entrepreneurship, including access to finance, incubators, and support for startups, as well as policies that encourage innovation and technological advancement.

9. Good Governance and Transparency

Good governance is essential for equitable development. We explore strategies for enhancing governance, including anti-corruption measures, transparent public institutions, and citizen engagement in decision-making processes.

10. Regional Integration and Trade

Regional integration and trade facilitate economic growth. We discuss strategies to promote regional cooperation, reduce trade barriers, and create opportunities for African nations to benefit from a larger market.

11. Environmental Sustainability

Sustainable development is vital for future generations. We explore strategies for environmental sustainability, including conservation efforts, renewable energy adoption, and policies that balance economic growth with ecological preservation.

12. Conflict Prevention and Resolution

Conflict can derail development efforts. We examine strategies for conflict prevention and resolution, including diplomacy, peacebuilding initiatives, and efforts to address the root causes of conflict.

13. Strengthening Legal Systems

Strong legal systems are essential for enforcing rights and contracts. We discuss strategies for strengthening legal systems, including judicial reforms, legal aid programs, and efforts to enhance the rule of law.

14. Youth and Employment

Youth unemployment is a pressing issue. We explore strategies to address youth unemployment, including skills training programs, job creation initiatives, and policies that promote youth entrepreneurship.

15. International Partnerships and Aid

International partnerships play a role in development. We discuss strategies for effective international cooperation, aid coordination, and partnerships that align with African nations' development goals.

Conclusion: A Vision of Inclusive, Equitable, and Well-Governed Africa

In conclusion, we envision a future where Africa achieves inclusive growth, equitable development, and good governance. These strategies offer a roadmap for African nations to overcome historical disparities, promote social cohesion, and create a conducive environment for sustainable progress. By implementing these strategies with dedication and vision, Africa can chart a path toward a brighter and more equitable future for all its people.

Envisioning a brighter future for Africa and its people

Introduction: The Promise of a Brighter Future

Africa, with its rich cultural diversity, abundant natural resources, and resilient communities, stands at the threshold of a promising future. This chapter explores the multifaceted dimensions of this future, envisioning a continent where equitable development, inclusive growth, and sustainable prosperity are not just aspirations but lived realities for all its people.

1. Inclusive Growth and Economic Prosperity

In envisioning a brighter future, inclusive growth takes center stage. We explore how African economies can diversify, reduce income inequality, and create opportunities for all, leading to increased economic prosperity.

2. Quality Education and Lifelong Learning

Education is the foundation of a brighter future. We discuss how a commitment to quality education, from early childhood to tertiary levels, can equip African youth with the skills and knowledge to thrive in an ever-changing world.

3. Empowerment of Women and Gender Equality

Gender equality is a non-negotiable pillar of a brighter future. We examine how empowering women and promoting gender equality across all sectors of society contribute to overall development.

4. Healthcare Access and Universal Health Coverage

Access to healthcare is a fundamental human right. We envision a future where healthcare is accessible to all, achieving universal health coverage and ensuring the well-being of Africa's people.

5. Sustainable and Green Development

Sustainability is at the heart of the vision for Africa's future. We explore how sustainable practices, green technologies, and conservation efforts can lead to a more ecologically balanced continent.

6. Technology and Innovation Advancements

The rapid advancement of technology offers immense potential. We envision a future where African nations are at the forefront of technological innovation and digital connectivity.

7. Strong and Accountable Governance

Good governance is vital for progress. We discuss the importance of accountable institutions, transparent policies, and the rule of law in shaping Africa's future.

8. Regional Integration and Continental Unity

A united Africa is a powerful vision. We explore how regional integration, cooperation, and the African Union's Agenda 2063 can lead to a more cohesive and influential continent.

9. Environmental Conservation and Biodiversity Protection

Africa's natural beauty and biodiversity are treasures. We envision a future where environmental conservation efforts protect these invaluable assets for generations to come.

10. Conflict Resolution and Peaceful Coexistence

Peace is a prerequisite for development. We discuss how conflict resolution, peacebuilding, and diplomacy can pave the way for a more peaceful and stable Africa.

11. Youth Empowerment and Leadership

Youth are the future leaders of Africa. We envision a future where youth are empowered, educated, and engaged in shaping the continent's destiny.

12. Cultural Preservation and Heritage Promotion

Cultural diversity is a source of strength. We explore how preserving and promoting Africa's rich cultural heritage can foster a sense of identity and pride.

13. International Collaboration and Partnerships

Africa's future is linked to global cooperation. We discuss how international collaborations, partnerships, and aid can support Africa's development goals.

14. Resilience in the Face of Challenges

Challenges are part of the journey. We envision a future where African communities demonstrate resilience and adaptability in the face of adversity.

15. A Vision of Unity and Solidarity

Solidarity among African nations is key to progress. We explore how unity and cooperation can propel Africa toward a brighter future.

Conclusion: A Shared Vision for Africa's Future

In conclusion, the vision for Africa's future is one of hope, determination, and shared responsibility. It is a vision where every African nation and individual plays a role in building a brighter, more prosperous continent. By embracing inclusive growth, sustainable development, and good governance, Africa can transform its potential into reality, forging a future that benefits all its people and inspires the world.

Conclusion: Illuminating Paths in Darkness

In the journey through the chapters of "The Dark Destiny of Africa," we have traversed the complexities, challenges, and triumphs that define the African continent. From the historical echoes of slavery to the persistent shadows of neo-colonialism, from the paradox of resource abundance to the plight of refugees seeking better lives abroad, from the grip of autocratic leadership to the fractures of ethnic conflicts, and from the degradation of the environment to the quagmire of corruption, we have explored the multifaceted realities that Africa confronts.

But within this narrative of adversity, we have also discovered the unwavering resilience of African communities, the determination of grassroots movements, and the power of local initiatives. We have witnessed the promise of education, innovation, and technology in shaping a brighter future. We have celebrated the potential for inclusive growth, equitable development, and good governance. And we have envisioned a continent where unity, solidarity, and shared responsibility illuminate paths out of darkness.

As we conclude our exploration, we are reminded that the story of Africa is not a single narrative but a tapestry woven from countless threads of history, culture, and aspiration. It is a story of challenges surmounted, of communities united, and of dreams pursued against all odds. It is a story that continues to be written by Africans from all walks of life, each contributing their unique chapter to the unfolding narrative.

"Illuminating Paths in Darkness" signifies not just the challenges Africa faces but also the resilience, determination, and hope that guide its people toward a brighter tomorrow. It underscores that the destiny of Africa is not predetermined but shaped by the collective efforts of its nations and individuals.

As we take leave of this exploration, let us remember that the story of Africa is ongoing, and its future remains unwritten. It is a story that holds the potential for transformation, progress, and prosperity. It is a story that challenges us to acknowledge the complexities, confront the adversities, and celebrate the achievements of the continent and its people.

In closing, "The Dark Destiny of Africa" is not just a narrative of challenges but a call to action. It is an invitation to engage with Africa's multifaceted realities, to support its endeavors, and to participate in shaping its future. It is a reminder that, in the face of darkness, the light of resilience, innovation, and determination can illuminate paths toward a brighter and more equitable destiny for Africa and its people.

178

Reflection on the multifaceted challenges highlighted throughout the book

As we reflect on the pages of "The Dark Destiny of Africa," a tapestry of challenges unfolds before us, painting a stark picture of the obstacles that have marked the continent's history and continue to shape its present. The multifaceted challenges woven throughout this book compel us to pause and contemplate the intricate web of complexities faced by African nations and their people.

1. Legacy of Slavery and Colonialism

The legacy of slavery and colonialism looms large over Africa, leaving indelible marks on its societies, economies, and political structures. The historical injustices of the past continue to reverberate in the present, influencing the dynamics of power, resource distribution, and international relations.

2. Resource Abundance and Economic Hardships

Africa's vast natural resources paradoxically coexist with economic hardships for many of its inhabitants. The mismanagement of these resources, coupled with external exploitation, has hindered economic development and perpetuated poverty.

3. Autocratic Leadership and Governance Challenges

The prevalence of autocratic leadership and governance challenges is a recurring theme. Many African countries grapple with leaders who remain in power for extended periods, often at the expense of democratic principles, human rights, and accountability.

4. Ethnic Conflicts and Regional Tensions

Ethnic conflicts and regional tensions simmer beneath the surface, periodically erupting into violence and instability. The complexities of ethnicity, identity, and historical grievances contribute to the fragility of peace and security in some regions.

5. Environmental Degradation and Sustainability Concerns

Environmental degradation threatens the continent's ecosystems, livelihoods, and future prospects. The consequences of climate change, deforestation, and pollution pose significant challenges to sustainability and well-being.

6. Corruption and Resource Exploitation

Corruption remains a pervasive issue, undermining development efforts and eroding public trust. The collusion between corrupt leaders, global corporations, and resource sales exacerbates the problem.

7. Refugees and Displacement

The plight of refugees and the displacement of people seeking better opportunities abroad highlight the urgent need for solutions to address the push factors driving mass migration.

Throughout our journey, we have encountered these challenges in their many dimensions, each revealing a facet of Africa's complex reality. Yet, in acknowledging these obstacles, we have also borne witness to the resilience, agency, and determination of African communities and individuals.

This reflection serves as a reminder that the challenges facing Africa are not insurmountable but require concerted efforts, innovative solutions, and shared responsibility. It is an invitation to engage with Africa's multifaceted realities, to support its endeavors for positive change, and to participate in shaping a future where the continent's potential is fully realized.

"The Dark Destiny of Africa" challenges us not only to understand the complexities but also to act upon them. It is a call to action for individuals, communities, nations, and the global community to collaborate in illuminating paths toward a brighter and more equitable destiny for Africa and its people.

A call to action for collective efforts toward positive change in Africa

As we conclude our exploration of "The Dark Destiny of Africa" and reflect on the multifaceted challenges that the continent faces, it becomes abundantly clear that Africa's journey toward a brighter future requires collective and concerted efforts. The complexities and adversities highlighted throughout this book call upon us to take action, to stand in solidarity with African nations and their people, and to contribute to the positive change that is not only possible but essential.

1. Support for Inclusive Growth and Equitable Development

We must actively support policies and initiatives that promote inclusive growth and equitable development in African countries. This includes advocating for fair economic practices, investments in education and healthcare, and measures to reduce income inequality.

2. Promotion of Good Governance and Transparency

Promoting good governance and transparency is vital. We can engage in efforts to hold leaders accountable, support anti-corruption initiatives, and advocate for transparent and participatory governance structures.

3. Investment in Education and Innovation

Education and innovation are transformative forces. We can support educational programs, mentorship opportunities, and initiatives that foster innovation, empowering African youth to shape their own destinies.

4. Environmental Stewardship and Conservation

Environmental conservation is a global responsibility. We can champion sustainable practices, support conservation efforts, and advocate for policies that address climate change and protect natural resources.

5. Advocacy for Peace and Conflict Resolution

Advocating for peace and conflict resolution is essential. We can raise awareness about conflict zones, support peacebuilding initiatives, and engage in diplomatic efforts to prevent and resolve conflicts.

6. Empowerment of Women and Gender Equality

Empowering women and promoting gender equality are central to progress. We can actively support women's rights, economic opportunities for women, and initiatives that challenge gender stereotypes.

7. Collaboration and Partnerships

Collaboration and partnerships at local, national, and international levels are instrumental in effecting change. We can engage with organizations, governments, and communities to collectively address Africa's challenges.

8. Investment in Youth and Leadership

Investing in youth and leadership development is an investment in the future. We can mentor young leaders, support youth initiatives, and advocate for policies that promote youth engagement.

9. Cultural Preservation and Heritage Promotion

Cultural preservation is essential for identity and pride. We can engage in cultural exchange, support initiatives that preserve cultural heritage, and celebrate the rich diversity of African cultures.

10. Advocacy for International Cooperation

International cooperation is crucial for addressing global challenges. We can advocate for responsible international partnerships, aid coordination, and support for African nations' development goals.

This is a call to action that transcends borders and backgrounds. It is an acknowledgment of our shared responsibility to support Africa in its pursuit of a brighter future. The challenges highlighted in "The Dark Destiny of Africa" are not Africa's alone; they are challenges that concern us all as global citizens.

By actively engaging with these issues, by contributing our knowledge, resources, and advocacy, and by standing in solidarity with Africa, we can collectively illuminate paths in darkness. We can help shape a future where Africa's potential is fully realized, where its people thrive, and where the continent's rich tapestry of cultures, histories, and aspirations continues to inspire the world.

Let this call to action be a reminder that positive change is not a distant dream but a shared endeavor, and it is within our collective power to make it a reality.

Encouragement to challenge the "dark destiny" and shape a more hopeful narrative

In the face of the challenges and complexities explored in "The Dark Destiny of Africa," it is essential to recognize that destiny is not a fixed path but a narrative waiting to be rewritten. While the shadows of history and the weight of adversity may cast a long shadow, they need not define Africa's future. Encouragement abounds for individuals, communities, and nations to challenge this "dark destiny" and craft a more hopeful and inspiring story.

1. Resilience as a Beacon of Hope

African communities have demonstrated remarkable resilience throughout history. This resilience is a beacon of hope, reminding us that even in the most challenging circumstances, people can overcome adversity, rebuild their lives, and forge a brighter path forward.

2. Innovation and Ingenuity

Africa is a land of innovation and ingenuity. From grassroots initiatives to technological advancements, Africans are harnessing their creative talents to address pressing challenges, develop solutions, and drive progress.

3. Youth as Agents of Change

Africa's youth are the torchbearers of transformation. Their energy, idealism, and determination hold the potential to reshape the continent's future. Encouraging youth participation in leadership and decision-making processes can amplify their impact.

4. Unity and Solidarity

Unity and solidarity among African nations have the power to foster cooperation, resolve conflicts, and achieve common goals. By working together, African nations can amplify their collective voice on the global stage and advocate for their interests.

5. Global Support and Collaboration

Africa's journey toward a brighter future is not a solitary endeavor. The global community has a role to play in supporting African nations' development efforts, respecting their sovereignty, and collaborating on issues of mutual concern.

6. Celebration of Diversity and Culture

Africa's rich cultural diversity is a source of strength and inspiration. By celebrating and preserving their cultural heritage, Africans can foster a sense of identity and pride, contributing to a more vibrant and inclusive future.

7. Education as an Empowerment Tool

Education is a powerful tool for empowerment. Access to quality education equips individuals with the skills and knowledge to lead change, challenge the status quo, and contribute to their communities and nations.

8. Environmental Stewardship

Safeguarding Africa's natural environment is crucial for sustainable development. Efforts to protect biodiversity, combat climate change, and promote eco-friendly practices contribute to a more hopeful narrative.

9. Commitment to Peace and Conflict Resolution

A commitment to peace and conflict resolution is essential for stability and development. Diplomacy, dialogue, and reconciliation efforts can prevent conflicts and pave the way for cooperation.

10. Advocacy for Human Rights

Advocating for human rights and social justice is at the core of a more hopeful narrative. By upholding the principles of equality, justice, and freedom, African nations can build inclusive societies.

The "dark destiny" outlined in this book need not be Africa's final chapter. It is an invitation to engage with the continent's complexities, confront its challenges, and celebrate its triumphs. It is a call to action for individuals, communities, and nations to contribute to a more hopeful and inspiring narrative for Africa.

As we embark on this collective journey of transformation, let us remember that destiny is not a decree but a story we collectively write. Together, we can challenge the shadows of the past and illuminate a path toward a future where Africa and its people thrive, and where the narrative is one of hope, resilience, and progress.

Acknowledgments:

In embarking on the journey to create "The Dark Destiny of Africa," numerous individuals and resources have contributed to the development of this work. We extend our gratitude to those whose expertise, insights, and support have enriched the content and the overall narrative.

First and foremost, we express our appreciation to the people and communities of Africa, whose experiences and resilience serve as the foundation for this exploration. It is their stories, their hopes, and their aspirations that have inspired this work.

We also acknowledge the invaluable contributions of scholars, researchers, and experts in various fields who have dedicated their time and knowledge to shedding light on Africa's multifaceted challenges and potential pathways to a brighter future.

Our gratitude extends to the global community for its ongoing commitment to supporting Africa's development and progress. The collaborations and partnerships forged in pursuit of positive change are a testament to the collective effort required to address the continent's challenges.

We would like to thank our colleagues, advisors, and mentors who have provided guidance and feedback throughout the writing process, helping shape the content and structure of this book.

Last but not least, we extend our heartfelt thanks to the readers of "The Dark Destiny of Africa." Your engagement with these pages and your commitment to understanding the complexities and opportunities facing Africa contribute to the ongoing dialogue about the continent's future.

This work is a collaborative endeavor, and your presence in this journey is a testament to the importance of engaging with Africa's multifaceted reality. Thank you for being part of this exploration, and we look forward to the collective efforts that will shape a more hopeful narrative for Africa and its people.

Recommended Books

DIGITAL
JOURNALISM
EMBRACING THE DIGITAL FRONTIER:
MASTERING THE ART OF
DIGITAL JOURNALISM
OSMAN KARAKAS
AWARD-WINNING JOURNALIST & LECTURER

A COMPREHENSIVE AND
PRACTICAL GUIDEBOOK
News Writing
Techniques
MOST COMMON MISTAKES AND TIPS
OSMAN KARAKAS
AWARD-WINNING JOURNALIST & LECTURER

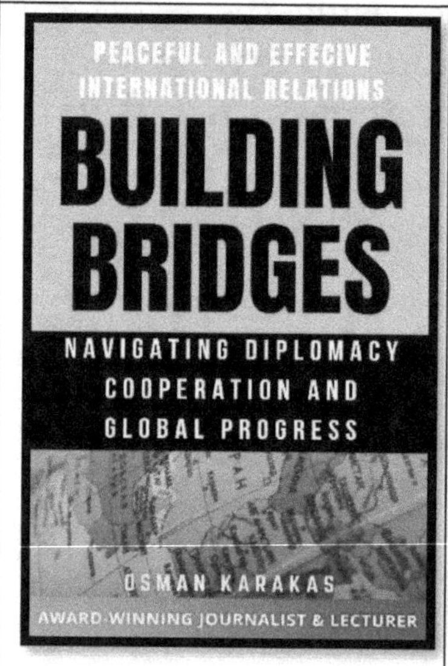
PEACEFUL AND EFFECIVE
INTERNATIONAL RELATIONS
BUILDING
BRIDGES
NAVIGATING DIPLOMACY
COOPERATION AND
GLOBAL PROGRESS
OSMAN KARAKAS
AWARD-WINNING JOURNALIST & LECTURER

MANIPULATION
OF MEDIA
NEWS
THE EROSION OF REALITY IN THE
MODERN NEWS LANDSCAPE
OSMAN KARAKAS
AWARD-WINNING JOURNALIST & LECTURER

COMPREHENSIVE GUIDE THAT EXPLORES THE
INTRICATE WORLD OF CRISIS DIPLOMACY
ART OF
DIPLOMACY
IN CRISES
NAVIGATING INTERNATIONAL
RELATIONS WITH FINESSE AND
STRATEGIC EXCELLENCE
OSMAN KARAKAS

THE SOCIAL
MEDIA
PARADOX
Citizen Journalism or
Social Media Terror?
OSMAN KARAKAS
AWARD-WINNING JOURNALIST & LECTURER

INTERNATIONAL
JOURNALISM
Global Perspectives of
International News
OSMAN KARAKAS
AWARD-WINNING JOURNALIST & LECTURER

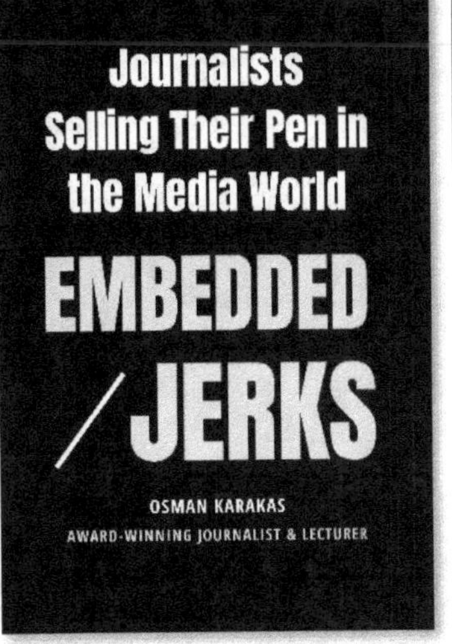

Journalists
Selling Their Pen in
the Media World
EMBEDDED
/ JERKS
OSMAN KARAKAS
AWARD-WINNING JOURNALIST & LECTURER

The collection of books is accessible for purchase on Amazon.com platform.